ALAN GARNER was born in Cheshire on 17 October 1934, and his childhood was spent in Alderley Edge, where his family has lived for more than four hundred years. He is a Fellow of the Royal Society of Literature and the Society of Antiquaries, and he was awarded the OBE in 2001 for his services to literature.

Praise for *Where Shall We Run To?*:

'In old age childhood memories become vivid again and it's the present that disappears behind a confusion of vivid fragments. In this book, Garner, now old, has faced that pattern and in place of the bewildering, wonky memory of old age, produced something precise and fresh as flowers. He has become – as we're told we must – as a little child'

FRANK COTTRELL-BOYCE, *New Statesman*

'Garner is one of Britain's greatest writers … *Where Shall We Run To?* is a book of witness. Its 16 chapters are tales that recall his childhood during the second world war. Its encounters are vivid and immediate, but it is also an examination of class and change in the England of those years'

ERICA WAGNER, *Financial Times*

'Every street, every house, every carved stone, mysterious well, dark pond and perilously steep cliff-edge is remembered and described, as Garner roams through it, with a succession of companions … Garner's detailed recall of so many characters and events is extraordinary' SUE GAISFORD, *Tablet*

'In this slight but charming memoir about his wartime childhood in Alderley Edge, Garner makes the Cheshire landscape feel fresh, while bringing a new perspective to a tried and tested literary form … and oh, what language'

BEN LAWRENCE, *Sunday Telegraph*

'This is a book very much about reading and writing, about the marks that we use to give life meaning, whether they are a tramp's chalk-mark on a wall or the comics and Arthur Mee's *The Children's Encyclopaedia* that allow young Alan to get past block capitals and closer to Real Writing. It is also a book written without a single scrap of hindsight, or rationalisation of the past. This, then, is a writer's memoir' BRIAN MORTON, *Herald*

'Written in a vivid first person, in a past tense that seems to belong not to seventy or eighty years ago but to a moment that has only just finished happening' *TLS*

Where Shall We Run To?

A
Memoir

Alan Garner

4th ESTATE • London

4th Estate
An imprint of HarperCollins*Publishers*
1 London Bridge Street
London SE1 9GF
www.4thEstate.co.uk

First published in Great Britain in 2018 by 4th Estate
This 4th Estate paperback edition published in 2019

1

Illustrations Credits: p.51: © Estate of Charles Keeping; p.97: Courtesy of
Hilda Gaddum; p.165: © Peter Wright; p.191: © Hazel Johnson; pp. xi, 7, 26,
31, 39, 55, 56, 70, 75, 82, 104, 112, 147, 171, 172, 182: © the author

A catalogue record for this book is
available from the British Library

ISBN 978-0-00-830600-7

Printed and bound in Great Britain by
CPI Group (UK) Ltd, Croydon

MIX
Paper from
responsible sources
FSC® C007454

This book is produced from independently certified FSC paper
to ensure responsible forest management.

For more information visit: www.harpercollins.co.uk/green

For Tom

Pancake Tuesday's a very happy day.
If you don't give us a holiday we'll all run away.
Where shall we run to? Down Moss Lane.
Here comes Twiggy with his big fat cane!

Contents

Bomb   1

The Nettling of Harold   6

Rocking Horse   23

Monsall   37

Porch   50

Mrs E. Paminondas   77

Mrs Finch's Gatepost   86

St Mary's Vaccies   93

Widdershins   103

Bunty   127

Bike   137.

Mr Noon   150

Half-Chick   161

DOWN MOSS LANE

Bomb (1955)   181

St Mary's Vaccies (1974)   187

The Nettling of Harold (2001)   189

Bomb

John and I were going up the Hough to pick water-cress in Pott Brook and to look at the anti-aircraft battery in Baguley's fields.

DANGER. DON'T TOUCH.

The notice was on the board outside the police station on Heyes Lane. A red arrow pointed to pictures of a high-explosive shell, small bombs with fins, a hand grenade; and there were some harmless-looking things too. And underneath was printed:

**IF YOU FIND ONE OF THESE, TELL
TEACHER OR A POLICEMAN.**

**DO NOT TOUCH IT, EVEN WITH
A STICK.**

AND DO NOT THROW STONES AT IT.

Pott Brook goes under Hough Lane, and we jumped
from the bridge into the field and began to look for
caddis fly larvae in the water.

Caddis larvae build tubes from grit and bits of leaf and twig bark to protect their bodies, with only the head and legs poking out. They showed the water was clean. If there were no caddis flies we didn't pick the cress.

It started to rain.

We walked along the bank to where the cress grew, and John found five tubes. We left the cress to be gathered on the way back and went upstream to look at the guns.

We were nearly across the field when we saw it.

It was on the other side of the brook, floating in a tangle of alder roots. It was grey, with a neck, and a black mark or letters or numbers on the side. We couldn't read them that far off. But we knew.

What must we do? There was no teacher to tell. It was holidays. It had to be a policeman. The notice said.

We ran back to the station. We looked at the notice again. There it was: on the left, third from the top. Should we tell our mothers first? It said: tell teacher or a policeman. We went in.

The sergeant was sitting at his desk, and he asked what he could do for us. We told him about the cress and the caddis and the thing in the brook, and we took him out and showed him the poster. He said we had sharp eyes, and we went back inside.

The sergeant opened a big book and began to write. Then PC Pessle came in. He was the policeman that saw us across the main road to and from school, and he had given me a broken police watch when I was two because I could tell the time. That's why my cousins called me Ticker.

The sergeant told PC Pessle what had happened, and asked him to go and check what we'd found. PC Pessle set off with us to investigate. It was raining hard.

We led him over the field at Pott Brook to where the thing was still bobbing in the alder roots. He got down into the water and broke off a dead branch from the tree. We shouted he mustn't touch it **EVEN WITH A STICK**. He told us to go back to the bridge and wait.

From the bridge we could see him bending down and poking. Then he climbed onto the bank, holding the grey thing with a neck and a black mark or letters or numbers on the side, just like the poster. John and I ducked below the parapet of the bridge, but PC Pessle told us not to be scared and showed us what he'd got.

It was a grey pot bottle, with words in black on the side:

VITAMIN BEVERAGES LIMITED

BREWED FROM HOPS, GINGER, ROOTS, SUGAR

WHICH ARE GOOD FOR YOU. ASK YOUR DOCTOR.

KEEP COOL.

PC Pessle went back with us to the police station and reported to the sergeant. They both said what good lads we were, and the sergeant wrote in the big book. John and I kept the bottle and we tossed for it. I won.

The Nettling of Harold

We were my cousins Betty and Geoffrey, me; Harold, his older brother Gordon, and baby Arthur; Ruth and Mary, sisters; and Iris. Betty and Iris were Big Girls, though Iris couldn't read. Arthur was there because he was in nappies and Harold had to look after him all the time. We were the Belmont Gang. I lived half a mile away, but my grandma lived at number 11, so I was let in, though I was a strug because I didn't come from Belmont. A strug was the word my uncle Syd and Harold's father used for a stray pigeon.

My grandma was old, and had wrinkly brown skin and silver hair and could skip better than the girls. She'd moved from Congleton to live in the village to be near her family because a war was coming, and number 11 was empty because the man living there had hanged himself in the lavatory.

Belmont had been built as four blocks of three houses in Potts's brickyard field. Each house was two up and two down, with a kitchen, and a garden at

The Belmont Gang, 1939. Back row, left to right: Betty, me, Gordon, Iris. Front row: Mary, Ruth, Geoffrey, Harold with baby Arthur

the front and a walled yard at the back. Later they had a lavatory added on in the yard. The cistern was in the kitchen to stop the pipe from freezing, and the chain went over a wheel and through the wall. We used to wait until people were sitting down and then pulled the chain to make them shout.

Next to my grandma lived Mr and Mrs Kirkham. They were old, too, but they kept themselves to themselves.

One day, the police had come from Macclesfield and told Mr and Mrs Kirkham they must move out because the house was going to be searched. They went to stay at number 11. This was before my grandma lived there.

The police lifted up the bedroom floorboards and the stone flags downstairs, and took out the built-in cupboards and made holes in the ceilings and tapped the walls and broke through the plaster and the bricks where they heard hollow sounds. And in each place they found money and jewellery and gold and silver. Burglars had lived in the house earlier and had hidden their loot there.

The police put everything back properly and tidied and redecorated the house, but my grandma said Mr and Mrs Kirkham were so upset they were never really happy again.

The allotments for the houses were separate strips, side by side, and my uncle Syd and Harold's father had their pigeon cotes there. We played on the patch of sand where the privies had been before Belmont was modernized.

When the war came, a brick air-raid shelter with a flat concrete roof was built, and it was dark, and the voices of grown-ups swore at us from inside when we tried to look.

There was an oak tree next to the shelter. We climbed onto the roof by putting our backs against the wall and walking up the trunk of the tree. The roof was our aerodrome, and we used to run round it with our arms out, preparing for take-off, and then have dogfights. Harold was a Messerschmitt 109, or a Focke-Wulf 190, because people said his great-grandfather had been a Gypsy. I was a Spitfire, because I could make the noise of a Rolls-Royce

Merlin engine. This meant Harold was always shot down and had to crash by jumping off the roof. He liked that. But I was too scared, and landed by hanging from the concrete and dropping into the grass.

I kept a hedgehog in a hutch on my grandma's allotment, and Harold and I gathered slugs to feed it. We picked the big black ones, and sometimes we found orange and grey. We popped the slugs with splinters of glass to make them easier for the hedgehog to eat, and we watched the innards, trying to work out which bits were which. We were both interested in Nature.

We were interested in everything.

I saved up by taking empties back to Mayoh's off-licence and collecting the tuppence deposit, and I once got into trouble with my mother for carrying the beer bottles in a basket without covering them with paper, because people could see. I bought myself Woodpecker cider with the deposit money, and spent some on carbide which Dobbin Brooks sold at his bike shop for making the flame of acetylene lamps.

Harold and I went fishing at the Electric Light Works, further along Heyes Lane, in a big concrete water tank. A woman had drowned herself there, but we weren't bothered in the daytime.

We put stones in an empty cider bottle, filled the bottle with water to just below the neck, and dropped lumps of carbide in. The lumps started to fizz as soon as they were wet, and we screwed the top on fast and tight and threw the bottle into the tank and watched it sink. Then we waited, excited; and the longer we waited the more excited we got; but we didn't make any noise.

We were waiting for the explosion to thud, and the dome of water and bubbles the same as the depth charges we saw in the newsreels at The Regal. Then the fish came up, stunned or dead, and we pulled them in with branches. They were sticklebacks. We couldn't eat them, because they were small and had spines, and I couldn't get the deposit back on the bottle; but that didn't matter.

The bottles had another scientific use.

We took them into the allotments where the long grass grew under the fruit bushes. We sat and turned the screw tops back and to, which gave a sound like the mating call of grasshoppers rubbing their legs on their wings. We were soon covered with grass-hoppers. They were on our clothes and in our hair, and they tickled our necks and faces, and tried to go up our noses and into our ears.

The allotments belonged to us. Although each house had its plot, the plots joined, and we moved between, following the fruit. We made our dens in the grass below the roof of leaves, which gave a light not like outside; and we golloped raspberries and blackcurrants and we talked.

We talked about why the sky was blue, why blood was red. Was it true if you put a hair from a white horse on your hand when Twiggy caned you the cane would break? Harold said stones in fields grew, because they came up every time a field was ploughed; but I said they didn't. My grandma had been a teacher, and she'd given me her Arthur Mee's *The Children's Encyclopaedia* of 1910, which taught in a different way from school. It asked and answered the questions teachers didn't, and had all sorts in it, but nothing about stones growing.

Why did stars twinkle? What was a rainbow? Why did lightning make thunder? How far off was the moon? How long would it take to get there in a steam train travelling at sixty miles an hour? And we asked our own questions. Where would they get the coal for the train from on the way to the moon? Why did the wind make leaves turn over before rain? Why did bubbles come on puddles just before the end of a downpour? Why, in the films at The Regal, did the spokes of car and wagon wheels go backwards? Did God watch us pee?

Why did nettles sting?

It mattered to me, a mardy-arse. I always made sure I knew where the dock leaves grew to stop the hurt. And it mattered most of all every year on Oak Apple Day, the twenty-ninth of May. Then, the boys used to run around holding nettles and stinging anybody not wearing an oak apple or an oak leaf. I got both ready the night before, so I couldn't be caught on the way to school.

Next to the air-raid shelter there was a great clump of nettles, Roman nettles, with purple stems. They were the worst.

I was standing by the clump with Harold, and I thought of the pain of one nettle. Here there were ever so many, hundreds. How much pain would that be? Would rubbing dock leaves on be enough to cure it? If one nettle made me cry, what would all these do? It was a big question; a scientific question. I must find the answer.

I moved behind Harold, put both hands between his shoulders, and pushed him in.

I'd not heard a boy scream before. It went on. It didn't stop. It wasn't Harold. I ran. I ran all the way home, up the stairs, fell on my bed, and yelled and yelled, still hearing the scream in my head, and cried and cried; but I hadn't got any dock leaves.

The next day, Harold called me a daft beggar and a mucky pup.

It was the time of the Liverpool and Manchester Blitz. My father joined the army to guard us against Hitler at Rhyl, and my mother and I went to Belmont every night to sleep with my grandma.

When the air-raid siren alert sounded we took cover in the gloryhole under the stairs. But that was damp and smelt of feet and old shoes, and after a while we stayed in bed. The brick and concrete shelter was never used.

I listened to the sound of the Dornier 17s, the Junkers 88s and the Heinkel 111s passing. The Heinkel engines made a low, beating noise. Then the Ack-Ack guns in Baguley's fields opened up and shook the furniture.

When the all-clear sounded, the Gang went out into Heyes Lane with torches to look for shrapnel. The glass in the torches was covered with black paper and had only a thin cross cut to show light; and we were careful not to point upwards, in case Jerry saw us.

Shrapnel was the bits of exploded shells meant to hit the bombers, and it had to be handled carefully because it was jagged and sharp. We wrapped the pieces in our handkerchiefs and swapped them in school at playtime next day. Hot-found ones were worth twice as much as cold-found; I don't know how we told the difference.

Harold was lucky one night and found a German incendiary bomb that hadn't exploded properly. It was in the gutter near Nancy Ford's shop, and it was like a bicycle pump, and a sticky white paste with a nasty smell was coming out of the cracks in the metal. We were all looking at it in the playground next day, but we made so much noise Miss Fletcher heard and came out and took it off us. We never did find another, and Harold was vexed for a long time after.

The air-raid siren in the village was the best in Cheshire, Harold said. It was always the first to sound the alert and the first to sound the all-clear. The rest followed, one after the other, at different times.

I told him it was because of the speed of sound, same as thunder after lightning. The sirens sounded all at once, I said, but we heard them later because they were further away. I'd shown him in *The Children's Encyclopaedia*, and how you could tell the distance by counting the seconds between the flash and the thunder. A second was as long as it took to say 'my-pet-monkey', and sound travelled a mile in five seconds. But Harold wouldn't have it. He agreed about lightning and thunder because he'd seen it in the encyclopaedia; but there was nothing about air-raid sirens; so we still had the best.

When the war came we sang in the playground:

'We're going to hang out the washing on the
    Siegfried Line!
Have you any dirty washing, Mother dear?'

It was one of the songs soldiers sang, and we heard it on the wireless and in newsreels at The Regal. In school, with Miss Turner, we sang 'Waltzing Matilda' and 'The Raggle-Taggle Gypsies' and 'The Ash Grove'. 'Waltzing Matilda' was a song from Australia about a man who stole a sheep and was caught and drowned himself and turned into a ghost. It had good words in it; words like 'swagman', 'billabong', 'coolibah', 'jumbuck', and 'tucker'. 'The Raggle-

Taggle Gypsies' was about a rich young lady who fell in love with a Gypsy and ran away with him and slept in the cold cold fields, and I wondered if she was related to Harold, or was one of the Gypsies that came and sat in our garden sometimes, but I never saw any that looked like her. 'The Ash Grove' was sad and made me want to cry.

One year, headmaster Twiggy had the whole school do a Carol Concert at Christmas to please Canon Gravell, with Miss Bratt playing the piano and him conducting.

Nobody liked Twiggy. He made us scared of him on purpose. And in the practices he never said we were any good but always how bad we were and how we didn't sing the words clearly. But that was because some of us weren't singing the real words at all. We were singing what we sang in the playground.

It was Harold's idea.

The knacky bit was to have only the Gang in on it, which was eight of us out of nearly three hundred in the school. If Twiggy did hear what we were singing he wouldn't be able to tell who it was.

THE NETTLING OF HAROLD

So we sang:

'While shepherds washed their socks by night
All sat around the tub,
A bar of Sunlight soap fell down
And they began to scrub.'

Then we sang:

'Hark! The jelly babies sing,
Beecham's Pills are just the thing.
They are gentle, meek and mild,
Two for a man and one for a child.
If you want to go to Heaven,
You must take a dose of seven.
If you want to go to Hell,
Take the blinking box as well!
Hark! The jelly babies sing
Beecham's Pills are just the thing.'

Then there was another.

'Good King Wences last looked out
Of the bedroom winder.
Silly bugger he fell out
On a red hot cinder.
Brightly shone his arse that night,
Though the frost was cruel,
When a poor man came in sight
Gathering winter fue-oh-Hell!'

And the best was to end with.

'O come, all ye faithful!
Butter from the Maypole,
Cheese from the Co-op
And milk from the cow.
Bread from George Cragg bakers,
Beer from Billy Mayoh.
O come let's kick the door in!
O come let's kick the door in!
O come let's kick the door in!
Twiggy's a turd!'

At the finish, Canon Gravell thanked Twiggy, not us. Then we broke up for Christmas. And the Gang laughed.

Soon after the war ended, though, Mr Ellis, our class teacher, told my parents I should go into Manchester and take a test. None of us knew what he was talking about. My class was being tested all the time, practising for the Eleven Plus exam. But my mother said because Mr Ellis was Cornish he had the Second Sight; and I liked him. A lot didn't. He let me read to myself in class while the others were reading aloud. He taught me to play chess and he taught me special punctuation. I liked semi-colons. He was strict, but not bad-tempered like Twiggy.

So I went to Manchester and took the test, along with two thousand other boys, in a room as big as The Regal.

A letter came in the post some time after, and my mother was waiting for me at the end of School

Lane when lessons were over. She told me I'd won a scholarship.

That evening, the Gang were playing round the sand patch. It was Ticky-on-Wood. Harold's mother came out of the house. Her face was different. 'Well, Alan,' she said, 'you won't want to speak to us any more.'

I didn't understand. I felt something go and not come back.

Rocking Horse

When I was five, my mother told me I was going to have to start school and I said I didn't want to. I wanted to stay at home and look after her. She said she'd waited since September so as not to spoil Christmas, but now I had to go or else we'd be summonsed. I shouldn't have to stay for school dinners, though. I could come home.

I said what about playtimes. She said I'd have to stay for them, but I could take the wooden curtain ring my father had brought back from one of the houses he was decorating, and the playground was bigger than our floor, so it would roll further.

My mother got me a new pair of clogs and greased the wooden soles with lard between the irons to stop the snow from bawking up and twist-ing my ankles, and we went to school for twenty to nine so I could meet the teachers.

Miss Fletcher was the headmistress of the Infants and she showed me my peg in the cloakroom where I had to hang my coat. It was number 17, the same number as my birthday. Then I met Miss Bratt, who was the teacher for the Second Year. She had a big head and grey skin and wore a box on her chest under her dress and her voice was hard to understand. That was because she was deaf, my mother said. Then there was Miss James, who was small and dumpy and had red cheeks. Her dress came right to the floor and she had to pull herself up to sit at her high desk.

Miss Fletcher took me to see the playroom, and I grabbed my mother's coat and wouldn't let go.

There were two horses, much bigger than me, made of wood and painted dapple grey. Their hooves were black with a gold line for horseshoes and their eyes were glass and bulged and their teeth were white and their nostrils and inside their ears were red and their manes and tails were real hair.

Miss Fletcher tried to lift me to sit on the saddle of one, but I shouted, so she put me down, and I shouted more because the horse had come alive and was rocking back and to and its nostrils were snorting over my head and it was going to eat me.

Miss Fletcher took hold of my hand, but I wouldn't let go of my mother. Then Miss Fletcher looked at me, and her eyes were like no one's eyes I'd seen before, and my mother got loose and went home. Miss Fletcher carried me into Miss James's classroom and sat me down in a desk next to a girl called Sheila, and Miss James told me to give over skriking.

The desk had two squares carved on the top, one for each of us. The squares were filled with other squares, ten across and ten down each side. The middle four squares made one big square with two lines from corner to corner, which made eight triangles. I didn't know what they meant, but counting them stopped me crying; and then Miss James was telling us a story about Three Little Pigs, and I listened, though I knew it already from my grandma.

The Infants. I am in the back row, two along
from Miss Fletcher, and Sheila is at the end on
the right of the second row from the front

Then it was playtime.

First we had to drink a third of a pint of milk through a straw out of a bottle. The milk was delivered by Johnny Baguley from up the Hough. He was thin and tall and wore his cap sideways, and he could jump over a five-barred gate in his milking coat and wellingtons without touching it. The milk was coloured light blue because he put water in, which was against the law, but he did it.

Miss James showed me how to push a hole in the middle of the cardboard lid and stick the straw through, and I knew how to suck the straw because that was how I drank when I was ill. Then we went out to play.

The playground was big and had a slope between the flat top and bottom parts. I'd never seen so many children or heard that much noise, and I was scared.

I saw Iris and cousin Betty from the Belmont Gang, but they were playing House with the Big Girls and didn't speak to me.

Other Big Girls were walking slowly in a circle clockwise, holding hands and singing:

'The wind, the wind, the wind blows high.
The rain comes pattering down the sky.
She is handsome. She is pretty.
She is the girl of the golden city.
She has lovers, one, two, three.
Pray can you tell me who is he?'

It made me feel sad. I didn't know why.

I couldn't see anyone else from the Gang. There were some boys playing Cigarette Cards. They were sitting on round gas mask holders made of tin, but I had to carry my gas mask in a square cardboard box, and I couldn't sit on that because I'd have squashed it. I'd asked my mother to let me have a tin one, but she said they were the wrong shape and would break the gas mask and I'd be killed if there was an attack.

Cigarette Cards was played by the first boy flirting a card forwards out of the side of his hand, and then the other boys took turns to flirt theirs to land on it. If a card landed on another then that boy won it and had another go and went on until he missed. But if the card missed first time they both stayed on the ground and the next boy tried. It was hard to flirt cards because the shape made them curve in the air and soon there'd be lots of cards lying on the ground. Then the knacky bit was to land a card on more than one and take as many as it touched until there was a winner. Girls didn't play Cigarette Cards.

The tin gas mask holders meant you could sit down in snow and not get wet. It had snowed the night before, and a slide had been got going down the steepest part of the playground, and I wasn't allowed on because my clog irons would have brogged it. So I went to roll my curtain ring.

I tried, but the snow made the ring fall over. Then I found a part next to the school wall where the snow had melted, and the ring went down all the way to the bottom, but one of the boys took it and ran off and wouldn't give it back, and the bell went for the end of playtime.

I sat next to Sheila and worried about my curtain ring. Then I got up and went to Miss James's high desk and pulled at her dress. I was crying again and she asked me what the matter was. I said I wanted a holiday. Miss James said she did too but she couldn't have one and nor could I, and she told me to go and sit down.

At dinnertime I went home and ate my bread and jam and said I wasn't going back to school. My mother said I had to, and she took me.

The first part of the afternoon was Sleep Time. There was an iron frame at the end of the classroom, with folding beds hanging on it. We had to lift them off the frame and set them out on the floor in rows. It took two of us to lift a bed. Michael showed me how to do it and helped me, and then I helped him. My bed was number 28, and I knew that was how old I'd be when I died.

We had to take our shoes and socks off and lie down and sleep while Miss James sat at her high desk and wrote in a book. Michael was next to me and his toe nails were long with thick white ends that let the light through.

If I lay on my back I could see two things. One was a round window near the ceiling made of different-coloured glass which had patterns I could turn into dragons. The other was an old-fashioned framed picture of a mother talking to her children. My mother had taught me big letters before I started school, so I could read what was underneath the picture. It said:

WE MUSTN'T SING ON SUNDAYS

BECAUSE IT IS A SIN.

BUT WE MAY SING ON WICKED DAYS

TILL SUNDAY COMES AGAIN.

When we got up, Michael had to lace my clogs and tie the bow because I didn't know how.

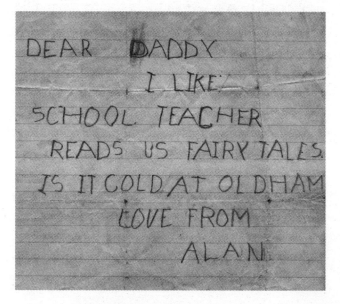

My first proper writing, January 1940

Miss James taught us for a year; then we went to Miss Bratt. We called her Polly because her voice sounded like a parrot. My mother said when children were in Miss Bratt's class they got too noisy to live with because Miss Bratt was deaf and everyone had to shout, and they shouted at home; and so did I.

Miss Bratt's room was not in the Infants part of the school. It was next to the hall, where we had Prayers, and it was horrible.

There were two windows, set between carved stone, high up, so we couldn't see out; and it was dark, because the branches of the holly and yew trees in the vicarage garden pressed against the glass all the time and weren't ever cut back.

Next to Miss Bratt's high desk was an iron stove. It burned coke, which was kept in the playground without any covering and was always wet, and the smell made us cough.

In front of the stove there was a wire mesh fire-guard with a brass rail round the top. If any of us got soaked with rain on the way to school we had to stand against the fireguard until our clothes stopped steaming before we could sit in our desks. The stove was so hot it made our legs blotchy red and white, and sometimes it made us cry, but Miss Bratt went on teaching because she didn't hear us.

And Miss Bratt wouldn't let any of us be excused during a lesson; so if we wet ourselves in class the boys had to stand at the fireguard to dry, and for the girls Miss Bratt took their knickers off and hung them on the brass rail. The smell of pee made us cough more.

One day, the smell was so bad I ran from the classroom, through the hall, out of the porch and up School Lane. Miss Bratt ran after me, shouting, 'Richard! Richard!', but I didn't stop and ran all the way home.

My mother was cross and said she'd tell my father, and then I'd get what-for. But it was the end of the afternoon, so she didn't take me back to school.

When my father came for his tea, my mother told him what I'd done, but he laughed when I said how Miss Bratt had chased me and called me Richard. I said I didn't know why she'd called me that, because she knew it wasn't my name. And my father laughed even more, and then he told me how my uncle Dick had done just the very same thing when he'd been in Miss Bratt's class, and she'd run after him shouting at him to come back, and she hadn't caught him, either.

My mother said my father must smack me, but he was laughing so much he gave me a hug and rubbed his whiskery chin against my cheek, and my mother went to wash the pots.

After Miss Bratt, we had Miss Fletcher. She was fierce, but her classroom was big and light, and she'd built a museum with rocks and fossils and sea shells and butterflies and beetles in a glass case. And on Friday afternoons she read real stories to us: *Winnie the Pooh* and *The House at Pooh Corner*, and she did all the voices differently. But the rest of the week it was Class Reading, and that was Milly-Molly-Mandy books, and we had to read them aloud in turn or all together. This was boring, except when

we had gas mask lessons, where we wore our gas masks the whole time.

We put our gas masks on by dipping our chins into the rubber mask against the tin breathing part, which had woolly asbestos in to stop the gas, and then pulling the elastic straps over the back of our heads with our thumbs to hold the mask fast.

The eyepiece soon misted up so we couldn't see properly, and if we breathed hard the rubber sides of the mask made rude noises, but Miss Fletcher didn't say anything.

I liked Miss Fletcher, even though I got into trouble.

One day, when there was an air-raid warning, I

lost my balaclava in the shelter and the teachers had to look for it after school.

The next morning, at the end of Prayers, Miss Fletcher called me out in front of everybody and told me what a nuisance I was. Then she lifted me up into the air with one hand by the back of my braces and spanked me. Because I was swinging in my braces it didn't hurt much, and I didn't cry, but it made me feel silly.

Afterwards, though, the same day, when we had Class Reading, Miss Fletcher gave me one of her very own books, *Alice's Adventures in Wonderland*, all to myself. And I sat and read it with my fingers in my ears and breathed hard in my gas mask so I couldn't hear that Milly-Molly-Mandy.

Monsall

I could read big letters but not little ones. I was being carried out of the house through the porch and I saw the bricks of the house on the corner of the road opposite and the iron plate painted white with the black letters STEVENS STREET. Then I was put down on a bed in a van with grey windows and tucked round in a blanket and a man in a hat with a shiny peak sat by me and held my hand and I went back to sleep.

The van was moving when I woke up and through the window I could see four black lines across the sky and they were dancing up and down and I asked the man what they were and he said they were the wires between telegraph poles. I watched them and went to sleep again.

There was a sharp pain at the bottom of my back, the sharpest worst pain I'd ever had and I woke up.

I was lying on my side on a stretcher in the open air next to a glass door. A woman in a blue dress and a white apron had her arms round me and another woman was holding a big needle and bending over the pain and telling me it would be all right. Then she helped to put me flat and I was carried up steps and through the glass door and along a corridor and the two women were holding my hands and talking to me and I was crying though the pain had stopped then I went to sleep again.

When I woke up I was in a bed. Someone spoke next to me but I couldn't move my head. I looked sideways and could just see one of the women sitting on a chair near the bed and I could smell smells I'd smelt before and I knew I was in Monsall.

I'd been in Monsall when I was two and had diphtheria which was one of my big words. Another was 'fumigated' because that was what was done to the house after I'd gone to Monsall.

Register Number ....

Monsall Hospital,

Newton Heath,

Manchester, 10.

I regret to have to inform you that

Alan Garner

Ward / 8

is dangerously ill, and should be visited with-

out delay.

D. SAGE SUTHERLAND,

Medical Superintendent.

18 · 3 1941

**Relatives are particularly requested, if they wish to see
the Medical Officers, to call at Ward 6 at 10 a.m.;
if this hour is inconvenient, at 8 p.m.
Sundays at 11 a.m.**

[OVER.

I remembered the woman was a nurse and she
told me she was going to look after me but I mustn't
move or try to sit up and she gave me something to
drink out of a small white teapot and put the spout

between my lips and I could swallow but I couldn't have moved if I'd wanted to. I had a headache all over. I couldn't move at all.

I went to sleep.

I kept waking and hurting and sleeping. The nurse fed me from the teapot in the day and in the night. Her voice and face and the colour of her hair kept changing but she never left me. I could see sky through a big window on the right and there was a small round window on the left in the door of the room. Sometimes a man in a white coat came and felt my neck and turned my head and felt my arms and legs and talked to the nurse and to other nurses and men that came with him and he smiled but he didn't speak to me. Then he left the room and the men and the nurses went except for the one that stayed.

It was daytime. I heard people talking outside the door but I couldn't hear what they were saying. I saw head shapes in the round window. They were moving from side to side pushing each other.

I said, 'Who's that?' and there was a noise and the nurse got up from her chair and went to the door and opened it enough for her to get through and I heard voices again and then they stopped and the nurse came back in and I started to cry because the noises had been too loud and hurt.

The nurse talked to me but I was still crying. She talked to me and held my hand. Then she held my wrist with her fingers and looked at her watch which was upside down on her chest. She put something under my tongue in my mouth and when she took it out and looked at it she said she was going to fetch something to make me feel better and went out of the room.

I stopped crying but I felt worried. I put my elbows down on the bed and pushed and sat up from the pillows and looked out of the big window.

The sky was blue with white fluffy clouds and I was looking down on a green lawn. A path went round the lawn and two people were walking away from me arm in arm. One was my mother wearing her best coat and hat and the other was my father in his soldier's uniform.

The pain in my head and neck and back and arms and legs jabbed and jabbed and jabbed and jabbed and jabbed and I fell in the bed and was sick.

I got better later; enough to be moved into another room.

It was big and had children in it. I didn't like them. They were noisy all the time, and those that were well enough to be out of bed and play were the worst. They ran around banging their toys; and they stopped me from reading my comics.

The very worst was called Arnold. His bed was next to mine on the right. He had yellow curly hair and big eyes, and he was always hitting the iron of his bedhead with a wooden hammer.

We had rice pudding to eat, and one day Arnold cacked himself and mixed it into his rice pudding with a spoon and ate it. I shouted for a nurse and told her what he'd done, but she laughed and gave him a bath.

My favourite comic was *The Knock-Out*. The best part in it was Stonehenge Kit the Ancient Brit, who was always fighting Whizzy the Wicked Wizard and his friends the Brit-bashers.

I couldn't really read before I was in Monsall. I could read the words in the pictures because they

were all big letters, but there was a lot more of the story below the pictures in both big and little letters, and I didn't understand those.

I lay in bed and looked at the words. Some of the big letters were in the pictures and in the story below, and some of the little letters were the same as the big. I tried to work out what the strange ones were by putting them together. Names were the easiest. 'KIT' and 'Kit' must be the same. So 'i' was 'I', and 't' was 'T'. Then once I'd got that I saw 'e' was 'E', 'n' was 'N', 'h' was 'H', and 'g' was 'G' in 'Stonehenge'. Then 'b' was 'B' in 'Brit-basher'. And so, one at a time, I learnt the little letters; and after practising over and over, in one moment I saw I could read everything. I was that excited I had to stop and lie down flat in the bed. I was shaking and couldn't hold the pages still. The sky was blue, with white fluffy clouds, and the sun shone on the barrage balloons.

Barrage balloons were tethered to the ground with cables for the cables to catch against the wings of German bombers in the Blitz and make them crash. The balloons were like fat silver sausages, and each had three fins to keep it steady.

Once, when I was at home, I heard a Spitfire engine and the sound of the machine guns. I went into Trafford Road and looked up and saw a barrage balloon had broken from its moorings and was drifting over the village and trailing its cable, and a Spitfire was trying to bring it down by shooting its fins and puncturing them so it fell gently without doing any damage or killing people. The pilot was circling round, being careful not to hit the body of the balloon, and I watched it sink until it disappeared over the Woodhill and the Edge.

As soon as I could read properly, Arnold didn't bother me much. Because I was reading, I didn't hear him. And when I was well enough to get out of bed my mother and father were allowed to come and visit me.

They could come for fifteen minutes, but they had to stand outside and shout through the window, and the window had to be shut tight.

I told them about Arnold and how he'd cacked

himself and how I could read now, and kept asking when I was coming home. And they laughed and my father said keep calm and carry on, which everybody used to say. And then the fifteen minutes were up and they had to go and it was somebody else's turn for fifteen minutes. We kissed through the glass and the glass was cold and we waved and I cried and they went home. And I went back to bed and read my comics.

Then one morning a nurse dressed me in my proper clothes and told me I was going home today. I asked her when, and she said as soon as my mother could fetch me.

The nurse took me to another room where there were toys lying around on the floor, and she said I must wait for my mother here.

It was a darker room than where I'd been, but there were chairs, and I could kneel up and look out of the window. All I could see was the sky and the wall of the next building, and the wind was blowing and it was raining and the drops ran down the window and everything was blurred.

I waited, but nothing happened, and the only sounds were the rain and the wind and people moving, but they were never my mother.

A nurse brought me a drink and some rice pudding. I didn't want any. I kept asking when my mother was coming. Soon, soon, the nurses said.

It was nearly three o'clock and my knees were sore, and the rain never stopped. I began to cry, and a nurse asked me what was the matter. I said my mother wasn't going to come. The nurse said she'd be here as soon as she could. It was a long way from right the other side of Manchester, she said, and the Blitz was doing that much damage lots of roads were still blocked; but my mother really was coming.

I said I knew she wasn't. It wasn't the Blitz. It was the rain.

This made the nurse laugh, but I told her it was true because when I wanted to do something or go somewhere my mother always said we could if it was a nice day and it didn't rain. It was raining now, and it wasn't a nice day.

The nurse tried to cuddle me. I knelt back on the chair and put my face against the window.

I didn't know how long it was, but a voice behind me asked if I was coming home or staying here. It was my mother. Her face was squiffy and it wasn't smiling.

Two nurses went with us to the door, and the air outside was full of tastes, and Herbert was at the bottom of the steps, standing next to his car.

Herbert had been the Best Man when my mother and father got married. He was a butcher, and he had an extra petrol allowance in the war so he could go to market. The car was big and the inside smelt of raw meat. I sat behind Herbert with my mother, and there was a dead pig in the back in case a policeman stopped us, and Herbert joked with me through the rain all the way home.

I had to go straight to bed and rest, but I didn't mind; and for a long time I had to stay indoors, and then not go outside the garden; and it was even longer than that before I went back to school.

I didn't mind. I had my books and comics; and my grandma gave me *The Children's Encyclopaedia*, which was five thousand three hundred and seventy-eight pages in eight volumes, including the Index. And I could read every one. Because I'd been in Monsall.

Porch

Our house was on Trafford Road where Stevens Street meets Moss Lane. It wasn't like any of the other houses. It was smaller and older, and had no garden at the front, only the footpath. That was because it had been a toll gate, people said. Big Sam Woodall, who walked without moving his arms, used to come and stare in at the window, but he was some kind of cousin to my father and meant no harm. There was a chimney at either end, a porch in the middle, and four windows, one in each corner. The window frames were made of stone set in the brick and had a stone pillar between the panes of glass.

The bedroom windows were so low, if the post-man arrived when we were asleep he knocked

'Birkett-and-Bostock's-brown-bread' on the door and my father opened the window and the postman handed the letters up to him.

There were three rooms downstairs. The one we lived in was called the House. That had the door to the porch and the road. The stone floor was covered with bits of linoleum, which were good for sliding on in my stocking feet, and rag rugs which my mother made from cut-up old clothes pushed into the webbing of a string net she knitted. The next room was the Middle Room. It had no furniture and I kept my budgerigar in a cage there. We used the Middle Room to get to the Scullery. The Scullery

was the room where the slopstone and water tap were and it had been added along the back wall. Outside were the coal shed and the lavatory, and a grid for the pipe through the wall from the slopstone. The grid had green jelly on it and I used to play with it when I was little. I didn't like the taste, though. And I once ate a grey slug, but it was gritty.

There was a big copper in the Scullery, set in brick with a fire grate under it for heating the water for Monday wash day and Friday bath night. The tin bath hung on a nail in the wall, and there was a dolly tub and a mangle for the washing.

The dolly was a pole with a T-handle at the top and a round piece of wood with three legs at the bottom. When I was big enough, I used to twirl the clothes in the dolly tub with the handle to make the dolly's legs work the soap in. Then I twirled with clean water to rinse the clothes. Then I turned the mangle to squeeze out the water, and tried not to get my fingers caught in the rollers. My mother hung the washing to dry in the garden, but if it rained she hung it on the clothes maiden in front of the fire in the House and steamed up the windows.

The clothes pegs were cut from willow branches, split at one end and bound with a strip of tin at the other. My mother bought them in bundles from Gypsy women, five to a bundle for sixpence. The women went from door to door along Trafford Road, and when they reached our house my mother let them into the garden at the back and gave them chairs to sit on so they could feed their babies, and she made them cups of tea. They thanked her and blessed her and sold her some pegs and went on their way.

The Gypsies were exciting. They had dark hair and skin and eyes, and they wore ear rings and bangles and bright clothes, even when the war was on. And they smelt more like cats than people.

Once, a woman was sitting and feeding her baby, and she stroked my head, lifted my chin and looked into my eyes. She told my mother I would grow up to be a big man, but she must watch out for trouble with my kidneys.

Soon after the women left, the men arrived, selling from door to door, each carrying a roll of linoleum on his shoulder, or a carpet, or a rug, or a piece of furniture, or a stick with rabbits hanging from it, skinned and gutted and without their heads, but with the paws left on to show they weren't cats. And when the men reached our house they didn't stop. I wondered why they didn't stop; and one day, after the women had left, I went into the road and looked at the house.

There was a chalk mark on a brick low down in the porch. It wasn't writing and it wasn't a picture; just a squiggle. But it hadn't been there earlier. So I remembered it. And if a tramp or the Singing Woman came begging in the village, I put the squiggle on the porch; and we were never bothered.

The fire range in the House was made of heavy iron, which my mother cleaned with emery paper and polished with black lead every week. There were three bars at the front, built up behind to make the fire high but narrow, so that coal and heat weren't wasted. On the left was a boiler for water and a hotplate, and on the right an oven with sliding dampers to control the heat. My Hough grandad Joseph had put the range in when he was a young man, and Joseph Sparkes Hall, my mother's great-grandfather's nephew, had invented it and shown it at The Paris Exhibition of 1867 as 'The English Cottage, or Test House'. He'd also invented the elastic-sided boot and had been Bootmaker to Queen Victoria and to the Queen of the Belgians;

and he'd written *The Book of the Feet*. My grandma told me that. And she had some of his letters and business cards and a photograph of him with another of his inventions.

Along the front of the range was a copper fender with a pattern of leaves on it; and at each end was a buffet, where I sat to read or to watch the pictures in the fire. I used to spit on the iron bars to see the spit dance and bubble and disappear.

The range fitted inside a big chimney space, and if I looked up it when the fire was out I could see the sky.

My mother raked the ashes every morning before lighting the fire. She lit the fire by putting a scrumpled piece of paper in the grate. Then she rolled a sheet of newspaper tightly from corner to corner to make a paper rod, and bent the rod in two places to make a triangle, folded the two crossed pieces over and put them through the triangle so the loose ends stuck out equal. She made three of these and laid them on the scrumpled paper together with sticks we'd brought from the Woodhill. Then around the top she put cinders that hadn't burned through properly the night before and added a few small pieces of coal; and then she lit the scrumpled paper with a match, and the fire soon brightened up so she could put bigger pieces of coal on to make a nest for the kettle to sit in to boil the water to mash a pot of tea for when my father came down for his breakfast. Then she got breakfast ready while the kettle boiled.

One morning, though, as the kettle was singing and starting to boil, a lump of soot fell down the chimney and knocked the kettle over. It put the fire out and nearly scalded me, and my father was vexed because he had to go to work without having his brew. My mother said he should have swept the chimney. And he said she must keep the fire out, which meant we had no hot water all day.

That night he came home with a brush and rods he'd borrowed from a chimney sweep, and he'd brought dust sheets from work. He covered the floor with the sheets, and the furniture and the walls and the fireplace, leaving a gap to push the brush through. Then he swept the chimney.

The head of the brush was round and the bristles stuck out sideways in a circle. The rods screwed into the head and then into each other in brass sockets.

My father stuck the brush up the chimney and twirled it and pushed to bring the soot down.

When he'd pushed the brush up as far as he could reach, he screwed another rod in and pushed again. The soot fell down the chimney into the grate, and some got into the room through gaps in the sheets and made our faces black.

My mother asked my father if he'd got enough rods to reach the chimney pot, and he said of course he had and it was easy now, so he must be nearly at the top. Then he fitted another rod, and pushed; and then he stopped. He pushed and twisted again, but the brush wouldn't move. He said he must have reached the chimney pot, but that didn't matter because it meant the chimney was clean and any soot in the pot wouldn't hurt, it was that high up.

He started to pull the brush back down, but it didn't move. He rattled the rods, but the brush was stuck. He tried again, harder, and again, and my mother told him to stop because he might loosen the chimney pot or break it, if he hadn't done already.

We went out to see.

The chimney pot was all right; but the rods were sticking out of it high into the air, and they'd bent over and down and the brush was all tangled in the telephone wires.

My mother began to nag at him, but my father told her to give over mithering. She'd said he must sweep the chimney, and he had.

There were two bedrooms in our house. The stairs went up nine steps through my room, with a rail and curtains around the top and two big cardboard pictures of Newfoundland Landseer dogs, and there was a door to my parents' bedroom. When I was ill I had a wooden cotton bobbin on a string and used to drop it from my bed on people's heads as they were going up. And in summer, if the weather was hot, I used to sleep across the end of the bed with my feet out of the window.

One day, when I was ill, an old man with white hair stopped to talk to me from the footpath. He said when he was a boy he used to play with the boy that lived here, and there were no stairs, only a ladder by the chimney of the fireplace. And when I looked I could see where it had been.

Something else about our house was different. It felt bigger inside than out. That was because the floors of the rooms were bigger, and the downstairs ceilings were lower, than the other houses in the road. Their high ceilings made them seem smaller too. And our bedroom ceilings weren't flat. They sloped up to the beam at the top, and there were more beams, upstairs and down, and the walls weren't straight. The humps and cracks and bumps made pictures, but the other houses had only flat paper with patterns on.

I loved the house, and I asked my mother if I could live there for ever when I grew up, and she said I could. But when my grandma got too old to look after herself we had to move into one of those other houses so she could be with us. It was fifty yards away, and I hated it because the walls were straight.

The most important part of the real house was the porch. The house roof had ordinary slates, but the porch had stone slabs, and a houseleek grew on the slabs.

The houseleek was there to save us from being struck by lightning. It grew on a heap of mossy roots and had leaves in round clumps. The leaves were thick and fleshy, with a prickly point, and the juice from them was good for curing sore eyes. Mrs Nixon had sore eyes and she used to come and ask for a leaf, which she squeezed and the juice dripped into her eyes and made her blink. When we moved, my mother took the houseleek and put it on the new coal shed. I didn't want her to do that, because it was more important to save the real house.

The porch was my den. It was inside and outside at the same time. I played there when I was little, and when I was older I put a chair in it so I could read, and count my stamp collection and look out at what was happening.

My mother donkey stoned the flags of the porch every week with a soft stone like a brick with a galloping donkey carved on it. She dipped the stone in a bucket of cold water and scrubbed the flags white all over. We got the donkey stone from the Rag-and-Bone Man, who came round on a flat cart drawn by a pony. He sat at the front corner, holding the reins and calling, 'Ragbone! Ragbone! Any rags? Pots for rags! Donkey stone!' and I gave him bits of rubbish and scraps and worn-out cloths, and he gave me a donkey stone for a swap.

Once, when I was in the porch, Mr Perrin, who lived down Moss Lane and worked in a cake shop, was passing by and he asked me if my grandad's name was Joe, and I said no, his name was grandad. That made him laugh. And he left a cup cake with white icing and half a cherry on top for me every day after, in the porch, round the corner where no one else could see it.

When the King died, the Prince of Wales became King Edward VIII. But before he was crowned he said he didn't want to be King, so his brother, the Duke of York, was King George VI instead. There was a lot of excitement, and my mother hung a cardboard picture in the porch showing the new King and Queen on a Union Jack, with the letters GOD BLESS KING GEORGE VI in gold.

A few days before the Coronation it rained, and the next morning the picture had peeled off and below it was another picture, the same but showing the Prince of Wales and GOD BLESS KING EDWARD VIII. My mother took it down and burned it.

Until the war started, on Guy Fawkes Night boys used to sneak into the porch and put rip-raps through the letterbox, and the rip-raps jumped around and my parents had to stamp them out to stop them setting the house on fire. And one year, my father heard a scuffling in the porch. The front door was heavy and opened outwards. My father crept to the door, listened, and waited. He heard a giggle, and he opened the door hard against the wall of the porch to trap the boys and shouted 'Got you!' But when he looked it was a courting couple squashed together and the young woman began screaming. He shut the door and switched off the light and we sat by the fire till the noise and the man's shouting went away.

I liked singing, and my grandma taught me Negro Spirituals, which she played on her piano. When Miss Fletcher heard about this she made me give a concert to the Infants after Prayers. I sang my favourites: 'Poor Old Joe', 'Swing Low, Sweet Chariot' and 'All God's Chillun Got Wings'. And then the choirmaster from St Philip's church heard about it and he tried to make me join the choir. I went to choir practice once, but I didn't like it, because I couldn't read the music and couldn't understand what he was talking about and some of the others in the choir kept changing the tune and I didn't know which was right, so I didn't go again.

A few times, my father came back from the pub with his friends, and if I was in bed he got me up to sing for them. I was shy, and the only way I could sing was to go behind the blanket that hung over the front door to stop the draught, and I sang there where I couldn't be seen. I sang the songs we heard on the wireless, not Negro Spirituals. I sang 'Toodleuma-luma-luma', 'Doing the Lambeth Walk', 'Ain't She Sweet?' and 'Ragtime Cowboy Joe'.

It was good when I sang behind the blanket because of the smell and the tickle of the doormat on my feet and the sound of the wind in the porch and through the letterbox.

One night, my father brought his friends home when the pubs closed, and they had bottles of beer and whisky with them, because my father had been called up to join the army the next day. He'd already said goodbye to my Hough grandad and uncles at The Trafford Arms.

I had to sing a lot of songs, and I got cold from standing behind the curtain and went and sat on a buffet by the fire to get my feet warm. I didn't like the smell of the beer and the whisky and the ciga-rette smoke, and the men were talking and laughing loudly and their faces were red. They laughed every time anyone said anything, but I didn't get the jokes.

One of the men, Fred Taggart, who lived down Moss Lane, wanted to go to the lavatory, and my father took him through the Middle Room to the

Scullery where the back door was. He didn't have a torch, and my father told him to follow the wall to the corner and then down between the Scullery and the coal shed to the lavatory door.

My father left Fred to it, but when he was in the Middle Room he remembered he hadn't switched the light on for the lavatory. The switch was in the Scullery, so he went and put it on and then joined the rest of us.

After a bit my mother said she was going to make a pot of tea for herself, and she took the kettle off the hob and went to fill it from the tap in the Scullery. But she came straight back and told my father to go and see if Fred was all right because she could hear a banging through the wall on the other side from the slopstone.

My father was gone a while, and when he came back he and Fred were laughing that much they were holding each other up, and Fred's forehead was bleeding and had to have a plaster.

What happened was Fred had felt his way along the wall in the dark and round the corner and down between the Scullery and the coal shed and had come to the lavatory door. He opened it, went in, and closed the door because of the blackout and felt for the light switch but he couldn't find one. And then he bumped his head against the cistern and the light came on. This was because my father had remembered and gone back to the Scullery and at that moment he'd flicked the switch, but Fred didn't know that.

When Fred had finished he couldn't see how to turn the light off, and because of the blackout he daren't open the door. So he began at thumping the cistern to put the light out, and that was what my mother heard.

This made everybody laugh even louder, and they opened more bottles of beer, and I went back to bed, but I couldn't sleep for all the racket, and I heard my mother go to bed too.

When my father joined the army the next morning, on Thursday, the sixteenth of January 1941, he left at twenty-five past seven. He didn't want to be seen off at the station. He opened the front door

and walked into the dark. My mot
and held each other. As soon as the c
the echo of his step left the porch he
army, not here.

When he came home on leave it was the other
way round. I heard his boot in the porch, and he
tapped 'Birkett-and-Bostock's-brown-bread' on the
door; and there he was. For me, he hadn't gone
further than the dark. But now he had a number. It
was 1768407; and he was called Gunner.

We never knew when my father was coming
home. Sometimes it was a surprise. If he found he
could wangle a pass for thirty-six hours, forty-eight
or seventy-two, he caught the first train out of Rhyl
or thumbed a lift. He didn't pay for travel, because
the ticket collectors at the stations wouldn't take
money from anyone in uniform. That wasn't
supposed to happen, but it did.

When he had official leave, we knew the day he'd
be home, but not the time. This was because my
Hough grandad and my uncles met his train and
took him to The Trafford Arms. Then he came and

My father home on leave, 1941

knocked on the door, and I opened it and he gave me a kiss and a hug. The first thing I always asked was when he was going back, because I needed to know how long it would be before he went out of the porch again. Then, one night, when he hugged and I asked, he said he wasn't going back. He'd been invalided out of the army because he wasn't fit enough to fight. Before the war, he was a painter and decorator, and the red lead in the paint had poisoned his stomach; so now he went to work at

Ringway aerodrome, painting camouflage, and had one day off every fortnight. He left home each morning before I was awake and came back after I was in bed, but I knew he hadn't gone away, because he used the back door, not the porch.

While my father was in the army my mother and I made a plan for the German invasion. I kept a bag of pepper by the front door, behind the blanket curtain. When the paratrooper knocked on the door I was going to throw the pepper in his eyes and my mother was going to hit him over the head with a poker and kill him. Then we were going to run upstairs and commit suicide by jumping out of the window.

One night, as we were getting ready to walk to my grandma's to sleep at Belmont, I heard a knock at the door. I went to the curtain and asked who it was. A man's voice answered in a language I couldn't understand. I shouted to my mother, grabbed the pepper and pushed the door hard open to trap him against the wall; but he didn't move, and the voice laughed and said, 'Hold your horses, Sonny! I surrender!' I looked, but there was nobody there; just the night. Then a torch was switched on and I saw teeth and the whites of two eyes. It was an American despatch rider leading a convoy of trucks through the village, and he'd lost his way. It was the first black face I'd seen.

He came in, called my mother 'Mam', gave me some chewing gum and some chocolate, and she made him a cup of tea. Then he thanked us both and tousled my hair, and he went back into the night.

Across the road from the porch was a street lamp. There was a metal plate at the bottom of the lamp post, but there wasn't a handle or a latch to open it. Instead there was a socket with six sides. I found a stick that fitted and put it in and turned it, and the plate fell off. Inside were different-coloured wires, twisted and tangled and going into different boxes. I fiddled with them, but nothing happened, so I put the plate back and locked it with the stick.

When the war started, because of air raids the lamp wasn't lit and that was when we had to have blackout curtains over the windows and the outside doors. The porch became a sentry box and I stood in it to guard the house from the German invasion.

I had a tin helmet and a double-barrelled popgun with corks on string. I stood at ease; then came to attention; then shouldered my popgun, marched across the road to the lamp post, about turned, one-two-three-away, marched back to the porch, halted, about turned, ordered arms, and stood at ease.

Then the Yanks came, and they stayed.

There were British soldiers in the village, but they weren't friendly and they wore black boots with nails in them which made a crashing noise when they walked. There was one kind soldier, Wally Deacon, who was billeted with my grandma. He was quiet and had brown eyes which always looked sad, and when I sat on his knee his uniform itched me.

The Yanks were different. They laughed and gave us comics and sweets and chewing gum and cigarettes made of white sugar with a red tip. When they were drunk they fought each other with broken bottles outside The Trafford Arms and Elsie Shaw's chip shop.

One day, when I was ill, a sergeant called Mervyn arrived in a Jeep driven by a military policeman wearing a white steel helmet with MP on the front, and he called up through my window whether I liked aeroplanes. The back of the Jeep was full of scale models of wartime aircraft, painted black because that's how they would look from the ground. They were used for aircraft recognition training, and he and the military policeman carried them to my bedroom and my mother hung them on sewing thread from the beams and I learnt all their shapes and names.

The Yanks' boots were brown and soft and made a swishing noise when they marched, and their uniform and shirts didn't itch.

When I was on sentry duty and heard them marching, swish, swish, along Trafford Road, I came to attention, shouldered arms, marched into the middle of the road, turned, presented my popgun and shouted, 'Halt! Who goes there? Friend or foe?' And the sergeant in charge ordered, 'Platoon! Halt!' and answered, 'Friend!'

'Advance, friend, and be recognized!' I shouted.

The sergeant came to me, halted at attention and produced his papers from his breast pocket. I examined them, gave them back to him, and shouted, 'Pass, friend!' shouldered arms and went back to my sentry box.

The sergeant ordered, 'Platoon! Forward ... march!' And on they came, swish, swish.

As they reached the porch, the sergeant ordered, 'Platoon! Eyes ... right!' Their heads snapped towards me and the sergeant saluted as they passed. I slapped the butt of my popgun in return. Then it was, 'Platoon! Eyes ... front!' and off they went down Trafford Road.

Then the sergeant ordered, 'Platoon! To the rear ... march!' And the platoon turned, and came back up the road.

'Platoon! Eyes ... left!' and the salute again. And the slap on my popgun.

The Yanks went. Their ship was sunk, and they drowned. From the porch, I kept watch.

Mrs E. Paminondas

Across the road at the end of School Lane were the school's two air-raid shelters, side by side next to each other.

They were long trenches dug into the ground, with a roof built over and covered with earth and grass. At one end was the way in, down steps and round a corner. The corner was to stop bomb blast killing us. At the other end was an iron ladder going up to a short tube with a lid on top. That was the emergency exit, in case we were trapped and couldn't get out by the steps.

Along the sides of each shelter were raised planks for us to sit on, and down the middle were slats for our feet. The shelters flooded, so our feet got wet. The only light was from the way in, but the corner made it dim, and most of us had to sit in the dark and we couldn't see who was sitting across from us.

When the air-raid siren sounded the alert, we stood up from our desks and filed out in rows to the playground. Then we made a long line, two by two, holding hands, with the teachers at either end, and walked to the shelters. We didn't run. There was no pushing allowed on the steps, and we couldn't bagsy being near the light. We sat on the planks and waited. We could talk, but only quietly, in case we missed the siren for the all-clear.

It was hot and cold and sweaty and shivery at the same time. The shelter smelt of slugs, and we couldn't help sitting on them, and there were live and drowned worms which the boys put down the girls' necks until Miss Fletcher told them to stop. Miss Fletcher had a deep voice and blue eyes and silver hair with a plait of golden red fastened round. My mother said she'd cut it off when her fiancé was killed in The Great War.

Marina could hear the tiniest noise and was always the first to warn us of an air raid, especially when we were in Miss Bratt's class and having Arithmetic, because Miss Bratt was deaf. The rule was that as soon as anyone heard the alert the whole school had to go to the shelters. The siren was on top of The Trafford Arms at the far end of the village. Marina could hear the brakes of the number 52 and number 29 buses at the stop outside Sammy Cohen Jeweller's; and they sounded a bit like the siren. When that happened we often sat in the shelters for more than two hours, but Marina was never grumbled at. We could be sure it was a false alert only if Mrs E. Paminondas didn't come.

We once had an Escape Practice Drill.

We went into the shelters when there was no alert, sat down and waited until a teacher blew a whistle. Then we had to climb the ladder to get out and escape. Denis went first because he was the strongest boy in the school, and could push open the iron lid at the top easily. Then we all followed, one teacher going next behind Denis to help pull us up.

The ladder was hard to climb. The sides were thin, and so were the rungs, but I managed, and it was good to put my face out at the top.

The other teachers came last, and the last in my shelter was Miss James. She'd been at the school for forty years and her coat was long and she wore a round brown velvet hat with a brim. And she got stuck.

We'd heard her grunting. Then her head appeared, and her hat was on one side and her skin all blotchy. I thought she looked like the Sphinx of Egypt in *The Children's Encyclopaedia*, with the long mound of the shelter behind her and her head right at the end.

Miss Fletcher sent some of the Big Boys into the shelter to help. They found Miss James's legs dangling in the dark and set her feet back on the rungs. Then they put their shoulders under her bottom and shoved. All that did was make Miss James shout. Her head was clear of the iron rim, but her shoulders were jammed fast.

The teachers bent down and talked to her, but nobody knew what to do next, and her skin was getting more blotchy.

Then Denis, who lived on a farm and knew how to move things, took over. He shouted down to the Big Boys to get a good hold of Miss James and steady her. He lifted her hat off and put it back tidy. Then he took hold of the iron rim of the tube and gently sat on the hat with all his weight. Nothing happened. He sat again, and bounced. Miss James yelled but didn't move. Denis told the Big Boys below to hold tighter and began to bump up and down on Miss James's hat. She started to sink. Her face disappeared and her voice was muffled. Then the boys below shouted. Denis stood up. Miss James's hat was still in the tube, but there was no Miss James under it.

The boys brought her out by the steps. Her hair and its bun were down to her shoulders, her coat was muddy and her face all dirt. Someone gave her her hat. She put it on carefully, and told Denis he was a good lad.

I can't remember a practice again.

When there was a proper alert we didn't mind. Although we were sitting in the dark and the smells and the wet, Mrs E. Paminondas was coming.

We knew really that Mrs E. Paminondas was my grandma; but now she was someone else.

When the alert sounded she put on her coat and her hat with its long silver pin and set off from Belmont along Heyes Lane to the shelters.

My grandma, Mrs E. Paminondas

She came down the steps and stood in the grey light, where we could see her, and she told us stories.

Mrs E. Paminondas had stories long and short, funny and frightening, magic and daft. We all listened, even those in Twiggy's class. But she never told us about Half-Chick. That was a special story, just for me.

She used to stop at an exciting part and say she was going to see how they were getting on next door, but she'd be back. And while she was gone, we had to think about what might happen next, and we'd see how right we were.

And she went to tell stories in the other shelter, and we made up the rest of the one we had. It didn't matter if we'd heard it before.

When she came back she listened to what we thought, and talked about it, and then went on to the end, putting in some of our ideas, so each time it was different. If the all-clear sounded and we were arguing with her, even if it was after school, we wouldn't let her go and we wouldn't leave the shelter until the story was finished. And Miss Fletcher said nothing.

The best story was 'E. Paminondas'; which is why we called her that.

E. Paminondas was a boy who went to his aunty and she gave him a cake to take home. He carried it in his hand, and by the time he got home it was all crumbs, and his mother told him the way to look after cake was to carry it under his hat.

The next time he went to his aunty she gave him some butter. He put it under his hat, and by the time he got home it had melted into his ears.

'Laws sakes, E. Paminondas,' said his mother, 'you ain't got the sense you was born with.' And she told him the way to look after butter was to cool it in water.

The next time he went to his aunty she gave him a little dog, and he dipped it in the river till it was cool, and by the time he got home it was dead.

'Laws sakes, E. Paminondas,' said his mother, 'you ain't got the sense you was born with.' And she told him the way to look after a little dog was to lead it on a piece of string.

The next time E. Paminondas went to his aunty she gave him a loaf of bread. He tied a piece of string round it and pulled it. And by the time he got home it was all gone.

'Laws sakes, E. Paminondas,' said his mother, 'you ain't got the sense you was born with. You never did have the sense you was born with. You never will have the sense you was born with.'

It was our favourite story, and every time E. Paminondas got home without the bread my grandma stopped, and we all shouted, 'Laws sakes, E. Paminondas, you ain't got the sense you was born with! You never did have the sense you was born with! You never will have the sense you was born with!'

When I read about E. Paminondas in *The Children's Encyclopaedia* I found his name was spelt 'Epaminondas' and he was an Ancient Greek general who had saved Thebes from the Spartans at the Battle of Leuctra in 371 BC. I wondered how anyone so daft could have grown up to do that.

Mrs Finch's Gatepost

Marina and I checked the gatepost every morning on our way to school.

It was while my mother and I were spending the nights at Belmont with my grandma when my father was in the army.

There was no gate to Mrs Finch's garden. We couldn't remember ever seeing one. But the stone post was there, and the wall; and set in it was an iron thumb latch, which had two positions: up and down. If it was up, there would be no rain that day. If it was down, rain was certain sure. So, as we passed, we checked, and changed the weather if we needed to.

Mrs Finch lived in a thatched cottage next to The Royal Oak on Heyes Lane. The cottage was built of brick and was yellow ochred. It was so old it sat below the level of the road. The garden was an overgrown orchard. Above her door was a brown painted sign with gold letters offering Refreshments and Teas with Hovis Bread. The door was always open, but inside was that dark it was hard to see.

Mrs Finch lived alone. She had company, though.

Cats sat in the doorway, ran in the grass and up the trees, walked along the stone wall and on the thatch, and we saw them moving inside the house, sitting on the furniture and in the windows, upstairs and down; and one cat, not always the same cat, was curled round the teapot in the middle of the table, keeping the pot warm in case someone called for a Hovis Tea, Marina said.

The stink made us hold our noses, even on the road.

Mrs Finch didn't scare us. And we didn't laugh at her. She was kind, and smiled. She should have been a witch, but we never thought she was. We met her on the road between her cottage and Rupert Warren's shop, where she went to cadge offal and scraps. The stink came with her and stayed after, as she shuffled along, always in a black coat and hat, always nodding and talking, though we didn't ask her who she was talking to.

One day, PC Pessle found her in the gutter at Joshua's Stile, opposite The Cottage Hospital. She was fighting over a cod's head with three tomcats, and an ambulance took her to Macclesfield. We never saw her again.

Some men from the Council came to get rid of the cats, but they couldn't. They drowned a hundred and twenty-three, Charlie Garner said, and then they lost count and gave up. Cats were running out of the door and jumping through the windows with kittens in their mouths. They made off and went wild on the Edge, and for a long time afterwards we saw big cats up there. When we were playing Tarzan they were lions.

I was always Tarzan, because I was the only one who could do Tarzan's war cry like Johnny Weissmuller at The Regal. And Sheila was Jane. But I couldn't climb, so I ran about on the ground while

the baddies went up the trees. That's when I used to
see the lions in the bracken, but I didn't run fast
enough to catch one and wrestle it to death, in case
I caught it.

I read *Tarzan of the Apes* twelve times, more times
than any other book ever, because my grandma's
book was old and the end was missing, and each
time I read it I thought I'd find the lost bit and
know what happened, but I didn't. What I did learn
was 'Kagoda' meant 'I surrender' in gorilla language.
And I told Tarzan stories of my own in the playground at school, and we acted them.

The only high place for Tarzan to swing from on
his liana ropes was from the ledge outside the railing
at the top of the cloakroom steps, so I jumped from
there and swooped with my arms up, gripping the
liana, round the girls playing Shake-a-Bed and
Queenie-o-coco as I chased the baddies with my war
cry. I knew it was liana because I'd read about it in
The Children's Encyclopaedia. One day, John got fed
up and gave me a Chinese Burn and wouldn't stop,
even when I said 'Kagoda.'

Marina was called after a princess who got married the year Marina was born. That was why there were other Marinas in the class.

Marina liked my Tarzan stories, and when we had Composition on Wednesday afternoons I wrote one in my Composition book and let her read it as I went along. I was still writing at playtime, but Miss Turner let me stay in so I could go on; and she let me not do Geography afterwards, too. But at the end of the afternoon she stopped me and wouldn't let me take my book home to finish the story. The next day I was ill in class with scarlet fever and pneumonia and pleurisy and didn't come back for a long time. That was another Tarzan story never finished.

When I started to get better I liked being ill. It meant that I didn't have to go to school and could lie in bed and think and read. What I liked best were *The Beano, The Dandy, The Knock-Out, The Champion, The Hotspur, The Wizard, The Children's Encyclopaedia*, my grandma's fairy-tale books, *The Chambers Twentieth Century Dictionary* and the *Rupert Annual*, though that was only at Christmas.

My grandma said a dictionary had every story that could ever be told, if the words were put in the right order; and if I was reading anything and came across a word I didn't know I must look it up in the dictionary, write it down, feel it in my mouth and not forget what it meant. So I did. When I went back to school I called a window in Composition 'opaque', and got a red tick for it.

I was ill a lot, but this time, when I was better and could play with Marina again, she showed me what had happened.

Mrs Finch's house had been pulled down. The orchard had gone. The wall had gone. The gatepost had gone.

The gatepost had gone, and the thumb latch had gone too. We couldn't stop the rain any more. Marina cried. I told her I'd read about weather while I was ill, and I explained how rain happened; but she didn't believe me. And I didn't, either. *The Children's Encyclopaedia* didn't say about thumb latches.

I wrote about the thumb latch to *The Brains Trust*, which was a programme on the wireless where people answered questions listeners sent in. They'd answered before, when I asked why the blade of the guillotine was slanted; but this time nothing happened.

Then Marina died.

St Mary's Vaccies

When the war came we had the vaccies. They were children moved out of the cities to be safe from the German bombers and they were made to live with the families in the village. The people in the big houses on the Edge didn't have any, unless they wanted them.

My mother had to take in a boy called Raymond. I didn't like him, and he didn't like me; and we had to sleep together in my bed. He wrecked my colouring pencils and skrawked my books and tore my comics and made me cry. In the end his mother came and took him back.

The first vaccies were a whole Roman Catholic school from Manchester, and there was only one

Roman Catholic family in the village, the Nolans, who managed The Regal, and the rest of us were Church of England or Methodist. In the cemetery, Church of England were buried on the right of the straight road down the middle and Methodists on the left. A corner of bushes was kept for 'Suicides and Other Faiths'.

Our school was a Council school, and the Roman Catholics wouldn't work with us for lessons or prayers, and there was a big muddle. But it was the start of the war, and nobody knew what they were doing; and because nobody was bombed the quarrel fizzled out and the Roman Catholics went home.

When the war really got going, the vaccies were from everywhere. But I didn't have to share with any of them, because I had whooping cough, measles and meningitis all at the same time.

The vaccies from Wallasey and London were townies, and a lot of them were from the slums. They were rough and had ringworm and impetigo and nits. Their clothes were in a worse mess than ours and didn't fit them, and a lot had their heads cropped in patches and stained with gentian violet and their faces were scabby and had yellow cream on, and their eyes were sticky. But Joan wasn't like that. She always wore a white blouse and black gymslip. We called her 'the clean vaccy'.

The worst was Alan, from London. He had a podgy face with slitty lids and he knew how to do real harm, not just hurt. He had my name, too, and I wanted him to die.

We couldn't escape in the playground, but out of school it was different. The vaccies weren't used to gardens, so we could hide. And if we were chased all we had to do was get into a field, because no townie, not even Alan, would risk finding a cow. But our real safe place was the Edge. There the trees and rocks and steep height kept us safe.

So the townies fought among themselves, and because they were gangs they couldn't join together to fight as one lot against us. But they taught us dirty swearing, though only one of us did it. We called him Kipper, because he smelt of pee.

Most of the vaccies stayed according to how long the Blitzes were on. The real vaccies were the Channel Islanders, from Torteval School in Guernsey. They stayed for five years, and the youngest, Madelaine, was only five when she came.

They weren't bothered by fields or the Edge, and we liked them.

They hadn't come because of the bombers but because Guernsey had been invaded by the Germans. They'd been brought out fast, with their headmaster Mr Le Poidevin, and they didn't know what had happened to their families and couldn't write to them or get letters. They were lonely and hard to talk to at first, and they could speak another language between themselves. But they played our games, not theirs, and only one of the boys was a bully. He was called Punny.

Punny scared me, until I found he couldn't read properly, so I helped him at playtime, and then he wouldn't let anyone touch me, not even Alan. Because Punny had a gun; or he said he had. I never saw it.

Punny lived with a family on Heyes Lane, but most of the Channel Islanders were all together in St Mary's Clyffe, one of the big houses on the Edge.

St Mary's Clyffe was built on a crag over a straight drop. It was on Woodbrook Road, which my Hough grandad's grandad, Old Robert, had helped to cut. The road had high rock sides with his pick marks on them, and it was dark and wet, with ferns and mosses growing, and the cobbles of the road were slippery.

The house was red bricks and blue bricks in patterns, with spikey tiles sticking up on the roof

ridges like on a dragon's back; and there was old-fashioned woodwork and sharp gables and a carving over the main door saying: GOD'S PROVIDENCE IS MINE INHERITANCE. We knew it must be haunted.

On Woodbrook Road, at the bottom of the garden of St Mary's Clyffe, there was a lamp post, and Madelaine used to climb up it into the garden to save her walking round by the gate, and slide down it on her way to school.

Madelaine was small, with deep brown eyes, and she was clever. She had two plaits and was a fast runner, and the only vaccy that laughed a lot, though I knew she was sometimes unhappy because she used to sit and look at her desk.

Miss Turner taught us, and everybody loved her. She had short hair, freckles, and she wore a green jacket and a green skirt and lisle stockings and flat shoes, and the first two fingers of her right hand were nearly black from cigarettes.

Miss Turner made everything interesting. On the twelfth of March 1945 we were allowed to write the

Madelaine

date in our workbooks as '12.3.45', because that couldn't happen for another hundred years. And she didn't have any favourites. I sat at the back of the classroom, and once I was so tired of not being chosen when she asked a question I was lying along my desk with my arm on the wall, not bothering to put it down, and walking my fingers along the bricks and staring out of the window. Miss Turner told me to sit up straight and stop fidgeting. She could see I was there, she said, and I was to put my hand up only if I didn't know the answer. But another time she let me draw the cross-section of a volcano on the blackboard in different-coloured chalks, just as I remembered it from *The Children's Encyclopaedia*. I got chased for that afterwards at playtime.

Every fortnight a van from Chester brought a crate of books to the school for us to choose to borrow and take home. We were supposed to have one each, but Miss Turner let us have as many as we liked, and Madelaine and I both read five a week.

In Miss Turner's class we started to have tests as practice for the Eleven Plus exam. One day, she set us an Intelligence test, and she said if we got the answers right the first letters of each answer, put together, would be the clue to a prize.

I finished the test before everyone else, and read the first letters downwards from the top. They were
COALSCUTTLEINSTAFFROOM

I ran from my desk, out down the corridor past the other classrooms, up the stairs to the staffroom. By the fire there was a coal scuttle full of coal. I got hold of it with both hands and lifted it off the hearthstone onto the carpet, but I had to put it down. It was too heavy to carry, so I humped it across the floor, onto the staircase, and banged it backwards down a step at a time, holding the handle in my elbows. Then, at the bottom, I dragged the scuttle along the stone corridor towards the classroom to get my prize.

The scuttle made a screeching noise on the stone, and I was sweating and hurting.

When I was nearly at the classroom Madelaine came out, jumped over the scuttle, ran off down the corridor and up the stairs. I shouted to her to come back because I'd got it. She took no notice. I dragged it on towards the door.

Madelaine and I arrived back in the classroom at the same time. I had the coal scuttle clue, and Madelaine had the bar of Cadbury's Bournville Plain Chocolate prize that was under it.

Miss Turner said very good; well done. And now take the scuttle back, please.

We knew when the war was ending, because all the soldiers left and we watched the Spitfires and the Hurricanes and the Lancasters and the Mosquitoes flying south, with three white stripes on each wing and the fuselage, which my father said meant we were going to invade France, because he'd painted them; but it was nearly another year before the war finished. And then I was ill.

The cheesecloth that had been glued onto my bedroom window to stop splinters of glass if a bomb dropped was peeled off and I could watch outside again with the window shut and make the weather-cock on St Philip's steeple and the whole of the steeple wobble by moving my head. It was the old glass of the window pane that did it.

I saw Madelaine running up Trafford Road. It was still school time. I opened my window and asked her what she was doing. She said she was going home, and ran on. I didn't see her again.

Widdershins

Privet leaves were green all year and tasted bitter, but hawthorn leaves were sweet and nutty when the buds were opening in spring, and we called them bread-and-cheese.

The privet hedges grew along Trafford Road, past our house, to the corner of Mottram Road, which was the road to my Hough grandad's house. From the corner it was hawthorn to the Hough and Mottram. I started to walk to my grandad's house when I was three, after I'd got better from diphtheria. There was a big, round white stone at the side of the road by the end of his garden, and it was a measured mile from the stone to the village. That was how I found how long a mile was and how much it made my legs ache.

Sometimes we used to go to see my grandad and grandma on a Sunday after tea. They lived in a house built of baulks of oak pegged together in squares, and the squares were filled with bricks or wattle and daub, which was mud and straw and cow muck on woven slats; and my grandad whitewashed the house every five years, my father said; and the roof was thatch.

Before I could walk, if it was dark, my father pushed me there in my black pram with a hood on it. He never pushed me in daylight, in case any of his friends saw him, because pushing a pram was a sissy thing for a man to do.

The part of the road where my grandad and grandma lived was steep, and when we left to go home my father used to run down with me in the pram from the gate as far as the Hough chapel.

One night, it was raining hard and I lay in the pram and my father began to run faster and faster, and I was getting more and more excited because he had never run so fast, and the pram was bouncing on its springs and I was shouting at him to run even faster.

Then there was a bang, and the pram upended and all the water in the apron tipped into my face and I yelled. Next, I heard my father asking me if I was all right, and I started shouting at him for getting me wet.

What had happened was my father, in the dark at the gate, thought my mother had hold of the pram, and my mother thought he had; and it wasn't until he said he'd take me they found out, and he caught up with the pram just after it crashed into the stone wall at the top of Hough Lane by

Henshall's farm. I wouldn't let him run with me after that.

I used to eat the privet and hawthorn leaves when I was going for a walk with my mother to the Woodhill. As soon as I nibbled bread-and-cheese round the corner of Mottram Road, even though it was only a few yards from home, I knew we were in a different place.

The gardens of the big houses began and went right up the hill to the top of the Edge. There was a wild patch behind a fence of chestnut palings tied with twisted wire, and in it was an overgrown well with an iron lid. Further along, on the left, was the Cricket Club, where the people from the big houses went to play cricket and tennis. Across the road, St Mary's Clyffe sat on a rock above the trees. Then there was Squirrels' Jump, the last of the houses, and after it the Woodhill came straight out of the ground beside the road.

The Woodhill was all beech trees, and their tops were so thick nothing could grow beneath them, except for patches of grass and bilberries near the road, and the ground was brown fallen beech leaves which people collected in sacks to make leaf mould to feed their gardens with. Sunlight came through the trunks like torch beams shone before the war.

There was a path along the bottom of the Woodhill, above the footpath on Mottram Road. When I was strong enough to climb up I walked on it, while my mother stayed on the footpath, and my feet were as high as her head.

When I was even stronger we both climbed through the beech leaves, which came past the top of my legs, to another path, half way up the hill.

This path was wide, but knobbly tree roots crossed it and I had to hop over them. And the path was dizzy and the hill was steep, with the trees all around us. My mother and I held hands and sang:

'We do not fear the gloomy wood.
We know the bears are kind and good.
Sing toora-loo, sing toora-lay.
We'll come again next Saturday.'

And when I was bigger we used to pull my black pram up onto the path and fill it with sticks and dead branches to light the fire with back home.

At the end of the Woodhill there was an old quarry. The wall sloped away and had footholds worn in it, and I could climb up them; but I was too scared to climb down and always slid back at the side on my bottom through the leaves and where the bilberries grew.

People said the quarry had been for the stone to build St Philip's church, but I didn't think that was true. The quarry was soft stone coloured red and white and yellow, but St Philip's was hard and grey.

The footpath changed to the other side of the road at the quarry, and a wall of the hard grey stone kept the field there from slipping down onto the path. My Hough grandad had helped his own grandad to build the wall. He was a stone-cutter, and the wall was the last job he ever did.

My grandad was ten years old, and it was his first job, the day after he left school. He left school early because Mr Consterdine, the vicar, said he was that clever he'd learnt everything he needed to know for what he was going to do with his life.

My grandad's grandad chose the stones and fitted them together, and my grandad chose smaller stones to make the date, 1886. The date was a secret of the Hough.

The Woodhill ended at the quarry, and the bottom of the Edge was steep fields, and a path of red sand with white boulders in it went up beside them into the woods. I couldn't climb this by myself until I was four.

The path joined a path that came from the right, and they made a path that went up for a short way to where the real Edge began.

It was a cliff leaning outwards, and beneath was a trough cut from solid stone, called the Wizard's Well, and every few seconds one drop of water, then two drops together, dripped into the trough from the cliff. Whatever the weather, wet or dry, the water dripped the same. It never changed. And above the trough, near the top of the cliff, the face of an old man with a beard was carved in the rock. People said my grandad's grandad had made it, and someone else a bit later had carved the words underneath:

DRINK OF

THIS AND

TAKE THY

FILL FOR THE

WATER FALLS

BY THE

WIZHARDS WILL

The path at the bottom of the cliff and round the well was slippery red clay, like salmon paste. That's what I called it.

A short way along there was another face, the same as the first, and it was by a split in the rock we called the Giant's Mouth. I could squeeze in and lie on my back with my nose up against white pebbles that sparkled in the light.

One day, when we were going past the Giant's Mouth, I asked my father how the pebbles had got fast there, but he didn't answer and told me to hurry up.

We were going to Castle Rock. It was along the flat path at the top of the Edge, and the front of it stuck out into the air above the fields and my grandad's house which were nearly three hundred feet below.

We climbed onto the Rock up a wooden ladder at the side. The jutting point of the Rock had wiggly grooves in it made by the rain, and it stuck out because it was hard stone, and beneath it was soft red and white, which had worn away. People had skrawked their initials in big letters in the soft part, dozens and dozens of them. But my father said my grandad, when the vicar told him he could leave school and get a job, he was that vexed he came up here and cut his whole name in Real Writing, the only Real Writing anywhere on the Edge. No one else could do it. My father didn't know where it was, but he knew it was there. One day, I found it and showed him, and he was that pleased he took his cap off.

I didn't like going near the point of the Rock because it made me giddy. I could crawl on my stomach and put my fingers in the wiggly grooves, but then I hutched myself backwards to safety, to a big bench on three stone stumps, and I sat on it and stayed there.

From Castle Rock on a clear day we could see Rivington Pike above Bolton, and Manchester, and Stockport, and to Lyme Cage and Kinder Scout, and the land all between was fields of different

colours. If we turned round and looked the other way we could see Bosley Cloud and Mow Cop and across to the mountains in Wales.

Before the war, we used to go to Castle Rock at night to watch the fireworks at Belle Vue Gardens in Manchester. When the war started, Harold and I went up once to watch the Blitz and the anti-aircraft guns firing in Johnny Baguley's fields in the Hough below. Then, after the war, at the end of the black-out, people from the village went to see the street lights being switched on. We looked in the dark as the night and the stars came; and then quickly, in patches, there were stars spreading on the ground beyond the fields, and the patches joined up and Stockport and Manchester were two big fuzzes of light and everyone cheered, and the real stars went out except for the bright ones, and we couldn't see The Milky Way.

My grandad's grandad had cut two faces at the Wizard's Well, but there were others along the lip of the Edge, always two, close together. Those that were easy to see had been smashed about the eyes and nose and mouth, and one of the two at Castle Rock wasn't a face at all any more unless we knew. There was only the shape of it left. But further along, towards the Beacon, the faces were too high up to reach from below and hard to see because they were against the light and grass hung over them from the path above. My grandad's grandad had cut proper faces, with hair and beards, but these below the path were a straight mouth with thick lips, a straight nose, big round eyes and a bald head. They went all the way to the Holy Well.

One head, near Castle Rock, was low down on the cliff and didn't have another like it. It was the face of a chubby man, with short locks of curly hair; and the eyes and nose and mouth had been hit, though not as hard as the rest of the faces. I thought he was Lord Stanley.

Bert Pretty was a friend of my father's; and he was what was known as a wild card. There were stories about him and his capers. And one day, when he was on leave from the army, he came with me and my father and we went to Castle Rock.

There was a gang of rough boys from Manchester making a racket and showing off. They'd fixed a rope round one of the bench stumps and were lowering themselves off the Rock to the path below then running back to the top and going down again, laughing and shouting and acting big.

We sat on the bench and watched them. My father was saying what he'd do if they were his.

When they were all on the path under the Rock, Bert Pretty got up and went to the edge and looked down. He shouted, 'Below!' And he jumped off.

My father and I climbed down the ladder and went round to the bottom of the Rock, and we found Bert standing on the path. All the boys were gawping at him and not saying a word. He'd jumped nearly thirty feet straight and landed on the path, which was only about eighteen inches wide there, with a steep slope beneath. But Bert was in the para-troops, and he knew how to land.

And the next thing, he took a handkerchief out of his pocket and blindfolded himself and set off to climb back. He went up the red and white rock and onto the hard overhang and to the top in one go. Then he took off his blindfold and called, 'Are you coming, lads?'

We left them, and my father laughed all the way to Stormy Point.

Another day, I was walking with my father on Castle Rock and I was looking at the patterns of the fields and the way the roads and lanes went between them. I asked him why Hough Lane had a bend in it. My father said, 'So it can get round the corner.'

When we were on our walks, my father told me things. The path went along the top of the steep lip of the Edge, and below it were the woods; and the branch of one of the larch trees reached close to the path. My father told me how, in The Great War, when he was a boy, a man had tied one end of a rope round the branch, made a noose of the other end, put the noose round his neck and stepped off the path right there and hanged himself.

Another time in The Great War, my father had been sitting on Castle Rock, he said, and the shadow of a Zeppelin airship had passed over his head and made everything go dark.

And he'd been on the station platform as a train went through pulling cattle trucks filled with Russian soldiers, and they all had snow on their helmets and boots.

The path from Castle Rock curved below a mound on the highest part of the Edge. At the top there were stone blocks scattered about. They were what was left of the Beacon, which had been built to give warning of the Spanish Armada and Bonny Prince Charlie and his army from Scotland when he marched across the Edge to invade England. And my father told me how the people living on the Edge went and hid in Ridgeway Wood below Stormy Point, and one boy who'd just got his first pair of britches took them off and put them in a tree so the Scottish soldiers wouldn't get them, because they didn't have any britches and had to wear petticoats instead.

The Beacon was blown down in a gale on Christmas Eve three years before I was born.

My father finished work at dinnertime on Saturday each week. And after dinner he nearly always went to watch football in Manchester. Then he came back for his tea, washed and shaved, put on his suit, and went to the pub. He went to The Drum and Monkey, then to The Royal Oak, then to The Trafford Arms, then to The Union Club. Then he came home, went to bed and slept until dinnertime on Sunday.

On Sunday morning my mother got up and cooked the Sunday dinner. She roasted a joint of beef with potatoes in the oven, and she boiled more potatoes, and cabbage and carrots and Brussels sprouts my grandad had grown in his garden up the Hough. And she made gravy and Yorkshire pudding, and a rice pudding with a brown skin on top.

Twenty minutes before dinner was ready, my mother knocked on the beam below the ceiling with the handle of the carving knife and my father thumped back on the bedroom floor with his foot. My mother served the plates to the table, which had a clean white cloth on it, and my father came downstairs, sat in his chair and ate his dinner. He mixed the rice pudding with the gravy and it looked horrible. I sat with him and had bread and jam, and my mother sat on the arm of a chair by the fire with her plate on her knee. No one talked.

After dinner, my father read the *News of the World* in his easy chair by the fire, and went to sleep until teatime. My mother cleared the table, took off the white tablecloth and put on a blue sateen one with tassels, and washed up the dirty pans and dishes. Then she went to bed to lie down, and I read my comics because I wasn't allowed to play out on a Sunday.

After tea, unless we were going to see my Hough grandad and grandma first, my father went to the pub and my mother and I listened to the wireless and played cards, always Strip-Jack-Naked, Rummy and Pelmanism. Sometimes we played Crib.

One Sunday, when I was five, my father sat down after dinner and read his paper. When he'd finished, he looked out of the window and said it was a grand afternoon and asked would I like to go up the Edge.

He'd never done this before on a Sunday.

We went along Mottram Road, up the Woodhill, past the Wizard's Well, to Castle Rock. My father was whistling and telling me things, and I held his hand.

We went on, not hurrying or going anywhere. When we came to the path to the Holy Well, I said I'd like to go that way, but my father said the path was mucky and we hadn't got the right shoes, so we climbed up towards Stormy Point and the Devil's Grave.

The Holy Well was one of my best places. It was a stone trough below a cliff, a bit like the Wizard's Well, but made of two slabs against two flat sides cut into the rock, and there was a little shallow dish, also cut, and shaped to a quarter of a circle.

The water didn't drip but trickled fast out of the bottom of the cliff and sparkled over bright green leaves by a wooden bridge made of planks and branches. The water ran under the path and down into a bog called Holy Well Slack, and then into a field at the bottom of the Hough and into my gran-

dad's garden and another stone trough where he got his water from.

In the bog there was a huge boulder that had fallen from the cliff and landed on an old woman and her cow and shaken all the houses in the Hough. It did that in the year 1740, my father said my grandad's grandad had said.

I could climb onto the boulder along the trunk of a pine tree that had been blown over, but I daren't go into the bog. I had once, and got in a pickle. I sank in over my knees and was stuck, until an old man heard me shouting and came and pulled me out by reaching with his walking stick.

Round the corner from the Holy Well was the Wishing Well. It was a round trough in front of a cave and water ran into it from a groove in the roof. People said my grandad's grandad had made it, and it was the only safe water to drink because of all the poison in the rock.

The water dribbled, but the secret was to find a leaf that fitted into the groove, and then it sent a spout you could get your mouth under and drink. Only one kind of leaf would fit, and it was a secret where to find it. After we'd drunk, we had to take the leaf out and throw it away, so strangers couldn't drink.

The Holy Well was a quiet place. It looked out over the fields, with the Edge curving on either side. And sometimes, if the weather was right, noises sounded strange. Then we could talk across the Slack and be heard on the other side and in the Hough.

I could see my grandad's house below and watch him working in his garden. If he saw me, and the quietness was there, he used to wave and whistle, and I heard him as clear as if he was on the boulder in the bog, and when I learnt to whistle I whistled too, and he waved again.

It was a special whistle he taught me. It was the whistle the donkey men used on the beach at Blackpool to make their donkeys turn round and come back when they were giving people rides.

There was another Hough whistle, which my father taught me. It was the first line of:

'Oh, can you wash a soldier's shirt?
And can you wash it clean?
Oh, can you wash a soldier's shirt,
And hang it on the green?'

If I saw any of my uncles or my father's friends, same as Inky Gezink, and whistled that, they'd answer by whistling the second line, and then they'd stop and talk to me.

Holy Well Slack had the only white clay on the Edge. It was under the leaf mould on the left down below the well and was another secret. We used it as soap to clean ourselves up before we went home after we'd been playing. And we used it to paint our faces when we were Cowboys and Indians.

We got our war paint from different parts of the Edge. Red was everywhere, but the best was at the Wizard's Well. Green and blue were in the clay at Engine Vein, an old copper and lead mine near the Beacon; and black and yellow were at Pillar Mine, below Stormy Point.

Anyway, on the afternoon when I was with my father, we went to the Devil's Grave.

Nothing grew on Stormy Point, not even grass. It was all rocks and pebbles and sand, from across the flat roof of the Devil's Grave right down the steep to Leah's fields.

The Devil's Grave was an old mine, too, but it was small and not dangerous like the others. It didn't kill people, and it was safe to play in and wasn't all dark. It was a sloping cave with a sand floor and the way down to it was a trench in the rock. There was a round hole in the roof, part blocked with a square stone so people wouldn't fall through the hole.

That Sunday, when we got to the Devil's Grave we stood next to the square stone and my father told me it was the Devil's Gravestone, and if you ran round it three times widdershins the Devil would come out and get you.

I asked him if it was true, and he said it was what he'd been told.

I asked him if I could have a go, and he said I could. So I set off running widdershins round the stone.

I ran once. Nothing happened. My father was looking at the view. I ran again. Nothing happened. My father still looked at the view. I set off again. Three times.

I said I'd done it.

He said I had and all.

A screech came out of the ground beneath my feet, and screams and groans and cackling and moaning, and pebbles flirted from under the stone and out of the trench, and sand and bits of twig, and there was a stamping sound in the cave, and more screeches.

I ran across the roof of the Devil's Grave back towards the path; but I hadn't gone far into the wood when I tripped over a tree root and fell on my face.

I lay there, shouting for my father, with sand in my mouth, waiting for the Devil's breath on my neck and his claws in my back. I waited and waited and yelled till there were only sobs left.

Nothing happened. Then I heard a sound. It was an ordinary sound. I looked through the bend of my elbow. My father and my uncle Syd were standing side by side at the Devil's Grave and laughing.

They'd planned it on Saturday night in The Trafford Arms.

My father was to get me to Stormy Point at three o'clock the next day, and uncle Syd would be waiting inside the Devil's Grave. They reckoned it was time, and I was old enough to learn the Edge.

Bunty

I had two stamp albums. One was 'The Strand Stamp Album arranged for the Reception of British, British Colonial and Foreign Postage Stamps, ample Provision being made for All Recent Issues, Thirteenth Edition fully brought up to Date, published by Stanley Gibbons, Limited, 391 Strand W.C.1 (opposite Hotel Cecil)'. That was for my collection. The other was 'The Famous XLCR Postage Stamp Album, published by Thomas Cliffe, Rhyl, North Wales'. That was small and I used it for my swaps, or sold them at a penny discount with every shilling.

I loved my stamps. Each one had a picture or a pattern with strange words on it, and sometimes just signs I couldn't understand. The words were in the language of the country they belonged to and had to be worked out if they weren't printed in English too. The only stamps without any words on them at all were British, because Great Britain had invented the Penny Post in 1840 and everyone in the world knew that, so British stamps didn't have to say where they came from.

I liked working out the names. Some were easy. 'Norge' was Norway; 'Belgique' or 'Belgie' were Belgium; and 'Nederland' was Holland because Holland was also called The Netherlands. But 'Poczta Polska' was harder, and I worked out it was Poland because I had a stamp postmarked 'Warsza' with the end missing at the edge, but it must be 'Warsaw'. And 'Helvetia' was Switzerland because there were stamps showing a man with a crossbow, and he was William Tell who'd shot an apple off his son's head.

But Tannu Tuva was the hardest. Although one part of a stamp had 'POSTAGE TUVA' on it I couldn't find the country on any maps, not even in my grandma's big *Philips' Handy-Volume Atlas of the World*. One stamp was an upside-down purple triangle and there was an elk's head and the value '1 TUG' and the word 'TbBA'. So, just as I did when I learnt to read small letters, I worked out it must be Tuva because it was four letters, beginning with 'T' and ending in 'A'. So 'b' was 'U' and 'B' was 'V'. But where Tuva was I didn't know, because it wasn't in stamp albums either. Then I found the Russian alphabet in a war magazine and saw I was right. But there was nowhere called Tannu Tuva in Russia, nor in my grandma's *Countries of the World* books.

The stamps had pictures of camels, and reindeer, and bears, and foxes, and turkeys, and lynxes, and men hunting with bows and arrows and dressed in furs and wearing pointed hats, so I decided it must be a cold country somewhere the other side of Russia and near Mongolia because the bows had big curves; and I went on collecting the stamps because they were triangle or diamond shapes, and I was interested in animals and liked finding out what they were. But some of the stamps with postmarks still had gum on the back and hadn't been licked, and that was strange.

Tannu Tuva became a magic land for me, and I wanted to find it and go there; but I never did.

I formed a stamp club to study stamps and wrote a set of Club Rules that everybody had to sign and swear to obey, and I made a tent for a meeting place by draping a blanket over the clothes maiden in the Middle Room where I kept my pet budgerigar.

Her name was Bunty. She had a yellow head and a green body, and she lived in a cage hung from a beam in the ceiling. I fed her on birdseed and wedged a piece of cuttlefish bone between the bars for her to nibble to keep her healthy and I changed her water every day. There was a mirror for her to look in so she wouldn't feel lonely, and a bell to play with, and she sat on a swinging perch and chirruped, and sometimes she climbed around the bars using her claws and beak to hold on. I was teaching her to speak, and she made a sound a bit like 'Hello', and always joined in when we were talking.

The only member of the stamp club was John, and he wouldn't sign to obey the Rules, so we lay in the tent and counted our stamps and swapped some, and then we took it in turns to be prisoners of the Cherokees and tied each other up with my mother's clothes line and were rescued by Crackerjack the Wonder Whip Man out of *The Dandy*.

Sometimes, but not often, Brian came to the club. He didn't join, because he didn't collect stamps, but we let him in.

Everybody liked Brian, though he didn't play much. One of his legs was a lot shorter than the other and he couldn't move fast. He had two rods that went down from his boot to an iron ring, and we all wanted to have one ourselves because it stopped him from being bullied. If anybody tried he crunched their feet so they couldn't walk, and he cracked coke with the ring, which we couldn't do with our boots or clogs.

The reason for cracking coke was to make hand grenades.

The coke pile was in the playground, heaped against the vicarage fence. There was a hedge of holly and yew trees on the other side so we wouldn't bother Canon Gravell at playtime, but there were gaps between the branches and we could peep through enough to see him sitting in his deck chair on a fine day wearing a cream-coloured jacket and a straw hat and reading his paper.

Brian cracked the lumps of coke to a size to fit our hands, and we held the lumps the way we'd seen soldiers and the Home Guard practising.

If we were right-handed we held the grenade against our chest in our right hand and pulled out the safety pin from the spoon, which was a spring lever we kept a tight grip on because when it was let go it set off the fuse which made the grenade explode five seconds later. If we were left-handed, we did the same thing, but with the grenade upside down. This meant we always pulled the safety pin out of the way so it didn't snag the spoon.

Then we stood ready, facing the enemy, and pointed our free arm in the direction we were going to throw. We held the grenade at arm's length behind us and lobbed it overhead to clear the hedge and land on Canon Gravell. Then we flung ourselves flat to avoid the explosion.

We always missed, but a few times we were close enough for the sound to make him twitch and look up from his paper. And once, when he was mowing the lawn, we saw him hit a piece of coke lying in the grass, and we heard what he said.

The next week, when he came into school for Special Prayers and told us to be good children and keep our hearts clean in Time of War, it was a gas mask practice day, but Canon Gravell didn't wear his though he had it with him. We said the prayers through the rubber sides of our gas masks, and he got angry with the rude noises we made, but we weren't bothered, because we knew what he'd said that other day the week before when he mowed the lawn.

Brian couldn't throw grenades, on account of his short leg, but he kept us supplied with ammunition. And in winter he made the coke into smaller pieces we could build snowballs around to throw against bullies. This worked, but there was always the danger the bullies could throw the coke back.

Brian liked the stamp club because he could talk to Bunty, and I was worried in case he was teaching her to talk better than I could do.

Then my mother was ill and had to go to The Cottage Hospital. My father was working at Ringway aerodrome painting camouflage, so I went and stayed with my grandma at Belmont.

Every day before school I called in at home to feed Bunty and give her water and clean her cage. And I put my hand through her door and she came and perched on my finger and we talked. And it was the same after school, when I spent more time with her because I had to put up the blackout curtains before I left for when my father came home from work at Ringway aerodrome, so he could switch the light on, and I was worried she'd be lonely in the dark.

One morning, it was very sunny. I set off from Belmont down Heyes Lane. When I got to The Cottage Hospital I waved to my mother because she had a bed next to a window and could wave back. Then I went along Joshua's Stile, past The Regal into Moss Lane and up to our house. I let myself in with a key and called hello to Bunty from the Scullery and went into the Middle Room to take down the blackout curtains.

Bunty was lying on the floor of her cage below her perch with her claws pointing upwards and her eyes were shut and she was dead.

I opened the cage door and touched her, then I ran all the way to Belmont and held on to my grandma and she held me and had that special grandma smell and I was crying and couldn't stop.

She said it wasn't my fault, but I said it was and I knew it was and I shouldn't have left her by herself alone in the dark. My grandma said it really wasn't my fault. Bunty must have pined, she said. I didn't know that word, but I didn't forget it, and I still couldn't stop crying.

My grandma put on her coat and her hat with the silver pin, and all the time she never let go of me. Then we went back home together.

She opened the door of the cage and lifted Bunty out and gave her to me so I felt the body was stiff and Bunty wasn't there any more. Then she let me carry Bunty in one hand and kept hold of my other, and we locked the house door and went back to Belmont. Her skin was rough and her knuckles were hard and swollen, but she held me gently.

We found an empty Heinz Salad Cream jar and I washed it and dried it, and I put Bunty inside. She fitted without squashing, and I screwed the lid back on.

Then my grandma gave me a trowel and we went into the front garden and I dug a grave and put the Heinz Salad Cream jar with Bunty into the ground and covered it with earth and we said a little prayer and I wanted never ever to have another pet again.

Bike

Mr Henshall died, and I got his bike, but I couldn't ride it. I didn't know how.

Mr Henshall was old and had a white moustache like my grandad's, and he delivered our milk. He carried the milk in four aluminium cans, two on each handlebar, and he lived near my grandad on Mottram Road at the corner of Hough Lane. He stopped at our house every morning and poured the milk from the can into the lid, to measure how much, and then from the lid into my mother's jug. Sometimes his grown-up daughter Margaret brought the milk on her bike, which was different because it didn't have a crossbar. Crossbars were for men.

Margaret had short black hair and bright red cheeks and was always smiling. My mother said I should marry someone like Margaret when I grew up because I was highly strung and I needed a farmer's daughter to keep me calm. I said I'd marry Margaret.

Mr Henshall always smiled, too, and so did a lot of other old people. There was Mrs Worthington, who was dressed in black, with a silver pin through her hat like my grandma's, and her coat nearly touched the floor. She pushed a big black pram with a hood, just the same as my pram, but it was full of pikelets she'd baked. She wore men's black lace-up work boots and walked in short fast steps. My mother used to buy me two pikelets for my tea and I ate them hot with Lyle's Golden Syrup spread over them. On the syrup tin there was a picture of a dead lion with a hole in its side and bees flying from it, and below were the words: OUT OF THE STRONG CAME FORTH SWEETNESS. My grandma said this was a story about Samson in The Bible where Samson was going to a wedding and he

met a lion and killed it with his bare hands. And
when he came back from the wedding he saw bees
had built a hive inside the dead body.

And there was Mrs Barton. She had a tall white
wooden cupboard on wheels with cart handles, and
inside the cupboard were shelves of cakes she made
with her husband. He had a white moustache, like
Mr Henshall's but bigger, and it stuck out sideways.
He carried his cakes in two wide baskets covered
with white teacloths, one on each arm, and he got
to The Royal Oak for twelve o'clock every day, when
the pub opened. He put the baskets on stone ledges
either side of the porch of the doorway and stayed
drinking till the pub shut at twenty to three. Then
he slept on a sofa in a back room until the bar
opened again at half past six. But Mrs Barton pushed
her cupboard round the village to sell her cakes, and
children used to run after her, singing:

'Roll along, Cakey Barton, roll along!
Let the wheels of your wagon sing a song!
While Jack Barton's drinking ale

All his cakes are going stale!

Roll along, Cakey Barton, roll along!'

One old man I knew never smiled. He was Mr Wright, who was a farmer and lived at The Wizard. He was kind and talked to me and gave me liquorice root sticks, which were the only sweets that weren't rationed. He wore a bowler hat and had the thickest moustache in the village, and he made jokes. But he never smiled.

Then Mr Henshall died, and Margaret gave me his bike.

I liked playing at Henshall's farm because I could go by myself and make dens in the haystack, and there was the frame of an old lorry in the orchard. It was rusty and had no wheels or seat or top, but it did have a steering wheel which turned, and I could stand and drive it.

At the back of the house there was a big wooden water butt to catch the rain from the thatch roof. The water was dark and smelt of slime, and I had to climb on two bricks to look. When I put anything in the water it changed colour as it sank and it disappeared before it reached the bottom.

The best things to sink were plates, which I took from Margaret's kitchen.

If I held a plate dead level on the surface and lowered it gently, so the water filled it without rippling and then let go and kept my hands still, the plate sank slowly and flipped and rocked like a manta ray fish in a film I'd seen at The Regal, and it changed from white to green as it went, until it was gone. Saucers were the same but quicker.

There was one thing scared me at the farm, and that was Margaret's dog. It was an Alsatian, and it was fastened by a rope through its collar to a ring fixed in the wall, and when it saw anybody it snarled and barked and jumped at the end of the rope. Margaret said it was only being friendly, but it wasn't.

If I wanted to get into the house through the front door I pressed myself against the stones below the garden hedge and there was just room for me to get past because the rope made the dog fall backwards. One day, though, as I was going towards the door and before I reached the hedge, the dog jumped at me with its mouth wide open, and I saw the ring fly out of the wall, and everything went different.

The ring stopped, and the rope hung in the air, and the dog floated and made no noise although I could see its teeth and down its throat and smell its breath. I ran past it into the house and slammed the door shut hard. Then I heard a thud against the door and a growling and a scratching at the wood and Margaret was holding me tight and I never saw the dog again.

My mother said she would teach me to ride my bike. I was worried, but John had a bike, and he could ride and he told me we could play speedway racing same as at Belle Vue, so I said I would.

The first thing my mother taught me was how to prop the bike upright against the kerb on one pedal so it stood by itself. Then I had to get hold of the handlebars and cock my leg over the saddle to the other side. This was because the crossbar was in the way, and I said if I had a bike like Margaret's I shouldn't have to do that and could get on easily, but my mother said it was a girl's way and I'd look a sissy.

When I was sitting on the saddle I had to put my feet on the pedals. I fell sideways, and my mother caught me and I leant against her on the saddle. The bike could freewheel, but she made me turn the pedals and we set off down Trafford Road.

I was still leaning against my mother, and I was wobbling because I couldn't hold the handlebars straight, but we got as far as Heyes Lane and then we came back. My mother had to push me uphill and I wobbled even more, but she made me press on the pedals as they came round.

We went to Mottram Road the next day because a lot of it was nearly level, and after a week of practising I could sit up and pedal with my mother holding me with one hand and the saddle with the other.

Soon I was able to pedal hard enough to go faster, and my mother had to run. We went along Mottram Road, under the Woodhill, up the bank to the

Hough Chapel, down Hough Lane, along Moss Road to Heyes Lane, past where Mrs Finch's house had been, past The Royal Oak, The Cottage Hospital and Joshua's Stile, round the corner into Trafford Road at the new Council Offices which had been built where there used to be a shop that sold bird-seed, past the end of Tyler Street and up to home.

We did this every day, and every day I got faster until my mother said she was out of puff, but she still kept running.

Then one afternoon, when we got to The Royal Oak, my mother clapped her hands and I saw she was running without holding me, and I fell off the bike and grazed my knees.

But after that I was all right and could go off on my own and explore where the roads went, further than I'd been strong enough to walk before.

And John and I could play speedway racing.

John's bike had tyres with treads on, but my tyres were worn smooth and didn't grip. John went from Tyler Street up Trafford Road, and I went the other way to where Trafford Road joins Heyes Lane. Then we set off full-pelt head-on towards each other so we reached Tyler Street together at the same time and John had to turn left into it, and me right, by leaning over, dragging one foot and skidding and sending dirt flying; and because my tyres had no tread they slithered and skidded better than John's and threw up more dirt. And we never crashed.

But I liked exploring best. Sometimes my mother came with me on her bike.

We rode to Congleton, where my grandma had lived at 47 Crescent Road before she came to live at Belmont, and I'd been born there. To Congleton and back was more than twenty miles, and it made my legs ache and my bottom was sore.

The people we visited talked about things I didn't know. And there was a man called Billy Jarvis who was the son of one of my mother's friends. He didn't seem to have a job, because he was always at home, but he had very blue eyes and he'd built a model steam train that used real coal and ran on lines, and he'd made all the parts of everything himself. He could also play the piano without music. My mother said the first time he saw a piano he sat down, hit a few notes and then could play any tune as if he'd learnt properly. But she said he couldn't read books. No matter of that, I liked him.

Because Congleton was such a long way we had to ride straight there and back without looking at things. My mother was interested in going, not stopping. There was a windmill water pump I wanted to see, but when I was with my mother I couldn't. So I used to explore by myself. And that was how I found churches.

They were all different. The first I found was Nether Alderley church. It wasn't like St Philip's next to the school, where no one was buried. It had a graveyard with old tombstones, some with strange writing on them which was Latin and Greek, and I wanted to learn how to read them, and I wanted to be buried there when I died.

And the church was different. It didn't have a steeple made of hard grey stone with a weathercock on top. It had a tower with battlements same as the castle at Tamworth where my great-grandad lived,

Four generations, Tamworth 1939

and the stone was yellow brown and old and worn. And there were painted shields everywhere inside.

The next church was Birtles. This had a tower, but it looked new outside because it was brick. Inside, though, it was full of carved furniture and panels and old stained glass from somewhere else.

Then there was the best church of all, at Marton. It was built of oak and plaster, black and white outside, and it was right next to the Congleton road, so my mother and I passed it every time, but we never stopped to go in.

When I went by myself I opened the door, and I was in a forest. The church had been built from trees. I could climb a ladder up to the bells and look down into the branches through a hole the shape of a four-leaved clover cut in the wood.

Near the church there was a lane, and when I explored it I found a farm. The house was old, with stone at one end, but next to the yard, by a midden, there was something older, I knew. It was an oak tree. It wasn't very tall, but it was wider than any tree I'd ever seen. The branches grew out and backwards, as big as trees themselves, with gaps between, and it was all hollow inside, without any wood except for the branches and the bark, and it was being used as a shed for farm machinery. And the roots were as thick as the trunks of ordinary trees. I'd never seen anything like it.

My bike showed me how the village and the Edge fitted into the rest. And when my grandma gave me her set of *Bartholomew's Reduced Survey for Tourists and Cyclists* maps I saw how it all worked.

I'd got *Philips' New Pocket Atlas of the World*, which had the countries in different colours, and everything belonging to Great Britain was red, but these other maps had roads on them.

I could see a black speck that showed where my Hough grandad's house was, and how Mottram Road met Trafford Road. And then I saw how the roads joined and made one big road, and I could ride from our house anywhere, to my great-grandad at Tamworth, if I wanted, and all the way to the sea.

Mr Noon

Mr Noon was the school caretaker. He had a brick shed inside the gates to the Big Boys' playground, next to the woodwork room. There was a ledge outside the shed, and Mr Ellis kept his thermometer on it, which he checked at playtime and then wrote the temperature in a notebook.

There were two playgrounds; one for the Infants and Big Girls and one for the Big Boys. Between them was a wall, with a door that was always locked. Each playground had a covered shelter for bad weather. The roof was on iron poles painted green, and the paint was worn thin by boys climbing. Girls didn't climb, because it showed their knickers.

Next to it were the lavatories. In the Infants' playground the boys' were stalls, which the girls passed going to their pans, and they giggled. But we had a way of getting even.

We used to have competitions to see who could pee over the lavatory wall into the playground. Norman was a Liverpool vaccy, and he was the best. He shot the other way, with his back to the play-ground, and could send a stream right into the girls' pans, which had walls but no doors, and make them scream. He was that good he aimed his first round to the furthest pan, dropping back one at a time as he lost pressure, with a pause between. We liked Norman.

The Big Boys' pans were used mainly for smok-ing, and every playtime Mr Ellis came out to sniff.

At the end of playtime, Miss Fletcher called the Infants and Big Girls in by ringing a brass hand-bell. It had A.R.P. on the rim, standing for Air Raid Precautions. Miss Fletcher was an air-raid warden after school. If there was a warning during the night, school began half an hour later the next morning, and sometimes an hour. It depended on how long the time was between the alert and the all-clear sirens. But it was no use pretending there'd been a warning if there hadn't, because Miss Fletcher would know.

To call in the Big Boys Mr Ellis used a whistle, which he blew three times. The first meant Stop Playing; the second, Stand Still And No Talking; the third, Get Into Line. And when we were all in our files we marched to our classrooms.

Our teacher in the first year of Big School was Miss Benison, who was tall and wore round glasses. She had pits in her neck where glands had been taken out for tuberculosis.

Once, Miss Benison had to be away from school to go to her mother's funeral. Her mother lived in Liverpool and had been killed in an air raid. When Miss Benison came back she finished the story she had been reading to us before she went. It was called *The Magic Faraway Tree*.

In Miss Benison's class we had Private Reading. That meant we could bring books from home, if we had any. I took *The Daily Express Film Annual* which had a photograph of Greta Garbo on the front. It was the only time Miss Benison scolded me. She picked up *The Daily Express Film Annual* from my desk and walked to the front of the class, waving it in the air, and she said it wasn't a book. The next time, I took *Stories of Tuffy the Tree Elf*. And after that I took *Newnes Family Doctor*. Miss Benison let me read both those books.

For Simple Physical Exercise we went into the playground, and Miss Benison held her arm straight above her head and we had to run and jump to smack her hand. I was the tallest in the class, and the second tallest in the school, and there was only me could smack Miss Benison's hand, because she was so tall too.

I was tall because I kept being ill and had to stay in bed. One year I grew seven inches, my mother said, and my Hough grandad called me a stick of forced rhubarb.

My grandma called me Half-Chick sometimes, because when I wasn't being ill I was always on the go and asking 'Why?' Most grown-ups just said 'Because'; but she didn't. And I didn't walk. I ran; or skipped. I skipped sideways, to school and back. And once I skipped sideways the measured mile right up the Hough.

If I was very poorly and couldn't read, my grandma used to come and sit by my bed and tell me stories. One was about Half-Chick. He wasn't like the others. He was born in half, and he was never still and wouldn't be told.

'He had only one leg one wing and one eye.
He left home. He made his mother cry.
He went hoppity-kick down the road, over the
    strand.
Hoppity-kick hoppity-kick to spy out the
    land.
The wind put him up on a steeple so he could.
And hoppity-kick hoppity-kick there he
    stood.'

My grandma said I was just like Half-Chick. I was a little autocrat, she said. I thought she said 'a little naughty cat', and I said I wasn't. That made her laugh, and it taught me a new word.

The next tallest in the class was William. He lived in the Back Streets, which were dangerous because the boys were rough and beat up anyone that didn't live there if they caught them. William's father kept Gort's chip shop, which wasn't as good as Elsie Shaw's. The fat had a sour taste and there was only one light, with no shade for the bulb. William said his grandad was Lord Gort VC, who was a Field Marshal in the army, fighting the Germans in Malta, but we didn't believe him.

What I didn't like most about the Big School was all the Big Boys played together and I couldn't play with the girls any more.

Mr Ellis took the Big Boys' Senior Physical Exercise. For this we put two squares of coconut matting together and had to stand with our toes against the edge of one and do a standing jump to land on the other. Only Kipper and I could do it, and Kipper was better than me because he was a year older.

He jumped in a funny way. He crouched with his hands together in front of him as if he was saying his prayers; then he jumped, and his legs and arms went out wide same as a frog's and came together when he landed more than half way along the second mat.

Kipper always wore a yellow jersey; and he held one shoulder higher than the other and turned his head, which made him look sideways when he spoke, though there was nothing wrong with him. He used to punch me on my backbone with the knuckle of his middle finger. That was one way I found I could run faster than anyone else.

Chelford was the next village, and every fortnight on Fridays the Big Boys from that school came to do woodwork. They were worse than Kipper. They lived on farms and were strong, and in the playground they ganged up to catch me. They twisted my arms and pulled my hair, and one put a lump of white dry dog dirt in my mouth. I was so scared I had stomach cramps, which made me cry and bend over when I walked. I told my parents, but my father called me a sissy, and said bullies were cowards when you stood up to them and fought back. It wasn't true. Not even Punny, the vaccy from Guernsey, could look after me on Fridays. I didn't know what to do.

But I worked it out.

If I waited at the far end of School Lane I could hear Mr Ellis blow his whistle. At the first whistle I ran down the lane to the school wall. At the second, I ran to the gates. At the third, I ran into the playground and joined the file.

The Chelford boys were the last out for playtime because they had to tidy their work benches, and I could get into School Lane and wait for the whistle for lessons to start again. But Mr Noon saw me. His shed was between the woodwork room and the gates. And after he'd watched me a few times he told me to come to his shed at playtime and hide in there.

Mr Noon was a big man with a round white face which was always the same. He never smiled or frowned. Most of the time he sat in his shed and mended things. He had a cobbler's last, and if anyone came to school with broken or leaking shoes he gave them spare ones to wear and mended theirs on his last before home time.

So I used to go and sit in his shed while he tapped nails and stitched seams in the light from the doorway, not speaking; then I'd dodge out and get into line at the third whistle; and nobody knew.

Mr Noon lived in Tyler Street, near to John.

Glyn Ridgeway lived in the Back Streets and worked for the Council. He did the jobs that didn't need him to be clever. And one day he came to get rid of the rats that were in the main sewer down the middle of Trafford Road. He opened the manhole cover by turning a key on the end of a rod with a handle on top. There was a deep shaft to the water, with iron rungs to climb on. But this day, Glyn Ridgeway didn't go down. He'd brought a sack of carbide, and he lifted the cover outside our house and poured the carbide into the shaft so it would mix with the water and the gas would kill the rats.

When he saw the water was bubbling and fizzing he put the cover back and locked it. But as he locked the cover he dropped his cigarette end down the shaft.

The gas exploded, and the force of the explosion went along the sewer so fast it couldn't escape sideways into the house drains. It went all the way along Trafford Road to the end. But at the end, the very last house on the sewer, in Tyler Street, was Mr Noon's.

Mrs Noon was sitting on the lavatory, and the explosion came up the drain and lifted the lavatory off its base and threw Mrs Noon into the air.

Mr Noon was at home and heard the crash and Mrs Noon screaming. When he got to her he found her on the floor among the pieces of the bowl, with the seat round her neck and her knickers round her ankles. I don't remember how we knew this last bit; but that was what everybody said happened.

Mrs Noon wasn't hurt, though she was under the doctor with nerves for a long time after; and Mr Noon retired. But by then the war was over, and the Chelford boys didn't come any more.

Half-Chick

The war went. We sang in the playground:

> 'Bikini lagoon,
> An atom bomb's boom,
> And two big explosions.'

David's father came back from Burma and didn't eat rice. And we were in Mr Ellis's class, the class of the Eleven Plus, which was the only way to escape being taught by Twiggy.

When my father had been at school and was a Big Boy he'd spent some of his time wheeling sand and cement and bricks for the extension of the school to make extra classrooms, the corridor, the stairs and the staffroom. The headmaster then had been Pop Kennedy, who taught by walking up and down the rows between desks playing a violin, with a cane hanging from his elbow, and reciting Latin and Shakespeare. My father remembered 'Deposuit potentes de sede et exaltavit humiles,' and 'Where is thy leather apron and thy rule?' Inky Gezink was always in trouble because he couldn't recite Shakespeare and said, 'Where is thy leather apron? And thy rule.' And Pop Kennedy caned him for it.

Twiggy was different. He taught by reciting 'The Pied Piper of Hamelin', 'The Charge of the Light Brigade' and the thirteen times table. He was fat and short and he shouted, and he had white hair, nearly bald, and cut into bristles. His neck was as wide as his head, and the back of it was folds, and the creases made eyes and a nose and a mouth, so when he was writing on the blackboard the creases moved up and down and seemed to be watching us and doing the talking.

Twiggy was a bully, though he never took any notice of me. Once, he came into Mr Ellis's room shouting and pulled Michael out of his desk by his ear and swung him round in front of the class. Michael was so scared he wet himself and the floor and ran out of school. Mr Ellis asked Twiggy to leave; and he did.

Mr Ellis was thin and tall, and he had a big forehead and a sharp red nose. He always wore a brown suit and waistcoat and shoes, and a brown trilby hat when he was outside. His bike had a rack over the back wheel to carry his brown leather case strapped down.

That year we had our first Guy Fawkes Night since before the war. My mother bought a ten-shilling box of fireworks from Allison's shop where I got my comics. Nobody else had as many fireworks as I did. She bought them weeks early, and I counted them every day and read the instructions and 'Light the blue touchpaper and retire immediately.' There were rip-raps and sparklers and Catherine wheels and whizz-bangs and Roman candles and bombers and two rockets and all sorts. They were the first bright colours I'd seen since I was five, except for the

Gypsies' clothes and the covers of *The Dandy*, *The Beano*, and the *Knock-Out* books. But soon after, the rims of plates and cups and saucers were coloured too.

On Guy Fawkes Night my father and mother took me along Mottram Road and we let off the fireworks below the Woodhill. We pinned Catherine wheels on the trees and stood the rockets in an empty beer bottle, and we laughed and shouted and I jumped in the dead beech leaves.

I'd been worried all weekend and all the week before, in case it would rain and spoil everything, and that Monday morning I sat in my desk and looked out through the window at the sky. The sky was blue, with white fluffy clouds, and the weathercock on St Philip's church in School Lane stood still, and it glinted.

The weathercock was on the top of the steeple, and if I was at the bottom and put my head right back and looked up when the wind was blowing the clouds from behind me the steeple and the weathercock seemed to be tumbling down, but I knew they

weren't. I showed Shirley, and she ran and hid in the school porch and wouldn't come out until Miss Turner told her it was all right and made me say sorry.

Next to the porch was the window of the hall. It was filled with diamond-shaped panes of glass set in lead; and when I stood to the side the weathercock was reflected in every one: a hundred and twenty-four half-chicks turning together.

The weathercock was bright gold because my father had gilded it fresh after the war ended. The steeplejacks had lowered it down for him, and I sat on its back. I hadn't thought it was that big.

And there it was now, high up again, glinting on the first Guy Fawkes Day since the war, while I worried about the rain.

Mr Ellis told me to pay attention. I thought I was in trouble. But Mr Ellis said it wasn't going to rain tonight. The temperature was forty-five degrees, and the barometer was Set Fair. So I'd have my fireworks.

Later, there were other fireworks we could buy, whether it was Guy Fawkes Night or not. They were plain white sticks with a stiff fuse and no instructions or writing on them. They were tuppence each. We called them Bangers because they were the loudest of all, as loud as those we'd seen used by the Home Guard and the army when they were training. Harold and I used to collect woodlice and slugs and fill a tin with them, light the Banger, put it in, screw the lid tight, and run. When the Banger went off we looked to see how many woodlice and slugs were still alive and whether the woodlouse armour made any difference, and how far the bits of the tin had travelled.

We couldn't put the Banger in too soon in case the burning fuse used up all the air and didn't explode. So we timed how long the fuse burned; it was between twelve and sixteen seconds. We reckoned we were safe to hold the Banger for eight seconds before putting it in the tin and there would be enough air for the fuse to burn.

All the boys had Bangers, but we were the only ones to experiment with them. Somehow Mr Ellis found out, and Bangers were banned and Allison's stopped selling them.

When everybody was present there were thirty-three of us in the class, including Denis. But Mr Ellis said he wasn't worth teaching and sent him to weed the garden of the telephone exchange outside the school, where he could see him from his high desk.

Then there was Shirley, and Sheila, and Angela, and Roy, and John, and me. The others called us 'Ellis's Pets' and we sat next to his desk. John and I sat together, and the difference between us was at the end of a lesson John's part of the seat was warm and mine was cold. John said it was because I was skinny, and I said it was because he had a big bum.

Mr Ellis taught us differently from the rest. They were given work to do and told to get on with it; and they had to be quiet. If any of them coughed, Mr Ellis said they hadn't got long for this world. But with the six of us he was patient and worked us hard, and we talked about different things.

The whole class was getting ready for the Eleven Plus exam. If we passed we went to grammar school; and if we didn't Twiggy had us until we were old enough to leave school and get a job.

Everybody practised taking tests. I liked the English and the Intelligence, but I didn't like the Arithmetic. I never had liked Arithmetic, and because I'd been ill so much I'd missed more than half of my time at school and the learning needed to understand sums. So I was never Top in that. In the rest I was, and always got 9/10, 9½/10 or 10/10, with a Red Triangle sticker in Miss Turner's class and a tick and VG for Very Good in Mr Ellis's.

One Wednesday morning it went wrong.

We'd collected our marked Composition exercise books from Mr Ellis. We wrote on white paper with blue lines and a red line down the left-hand side for a margin, and the covers were grey, with Cheshire Education Committee and SAFETY FIRST! and a list of DANGER DONT'S! printed on the front cover.

My composition was on the last page in the book. It followed a composition where I'd written about constellations and stars which I'd read about in *The Children's Encyclopaedia* and then found them in the sky, and I'd been given a tick and 10/10. I had 10/10 now; but I saw the difference.

I was used to writing about 'A Day in the Life of a Penny' and 'How to Clean a Pair of Shoes'; and sometimes we were allowed to write stories for ourselves. Now, though, I looked at what I'd written, and because it was the last and on the last page I saw what it said. This was what the work and the learning had been for.

I'd written a practice letter to apply for a job. Mr Ellis had put on the blackboard how we should write it, and what words we should use, and how we should say something interesting about ourselves, and how we should sign it. And I'd written:

Dear Sirs,

In this morning's 'Daily Express' I saw your advertisement concerning the vacancy in your counting house, and, gentlemen I would like to offer my application for the situation. I am now attending Alderley Edge Council School, and have been quite successful in English.

Hoping this will receive your attention,

I beg to remain,

Your most humble and obedient servant ...

And then my name.

being a group of stars that form a picture. ✓
Among the many constellations are :—
Ursa major, Ursa minor, Pisces, Orion, The
Plough, The Archer, The Hunter, Cassiopia,
The Lire, The Serpent, and The Scorpion.

> 'The Cottage',
> Trafford Rd.
> Alderley Edge.
> Nr Manc, ✓
>
> 6. 3. 46.

'Dear Sirs,
        In this morning's "Daily Express" I
saw your advertisment concerning the vacancy
in your counting house, and, gentlemen I would
like to offer my application for the situation. I am
now attending Alderly Edge Council School, and
have been quite succeful in English.
        Hoping this will receive your attention,
        I beg to remain,
            your most humble and obedient servant
            Alan Garner

But I wasn't begging. I couldn't remain what I
hadn't been. I didn't want to be humble and obedient. I wasn't a servant.

For a while, when I was little, I'd wanted to be a
man that worked down drains. Then later, Harold

and I had sat on Castle Rock and watched Barracuda dive-bombers from Ringway aerodrome being tested, and how they stood on their tails and climbed, flipped over and came straight down at full power as if they were going to crash, but always pulled out in time; and I wanted to be a test pilot. Now I didn't know what I wanted, but it wasn't a humble and obedient servant.

Miss Turner and Mr Ellis, the very best teachers, had tricked me with their Red Triangles, VGs and 10/10s. So, at the very bottom of the book's back cover, opposite the letter asking for the job as a vacancy in a counting house, I wrote in tiny letters, In Two days I Sit for the Manchester Grammar School Scholarship.

Then I looked at what I'd done, and I panicked.

When we reached the end of an exercise book we had to take it up to Mr Ellis for him to initial it and give us a new one. I had to do that now. And my tiny writing inside the cover got bigger and bigger. I tore the bottom of the cover where it met the page, folded it over the writing, made a tight crease and took it to Mr Ellis's desk. He scribbled his initials JHE in red pencil on the cover and gave it back to me, along with a new exercise book; and he smiled, though he didn't usually. He must have seen what I'd done.

Before we sat the Eleven Plus exam, which I had to take even though by then I'd got the other scholarship, Mr Ellis explained what would happen.

We were going to sit at our desks with the exam paper face down so we couldn't read the questions, and we wouldn't be allowed to talk. Mr Ellis would be there, but he wasn't allowed to say anything in case he helped us. An old man, Dr Heywood, was in charge, to tell us when to turn the paper over and start, and also when to stop at the end of the exam time, and to make sure there was no cheating. If we finished answering the questions early we should check everything until Dr Heywood said the time was up. Then we had to put our pens down at once and sit up and not talk until Dr Heywood told us we could. But, so we'd know how much time was left towards the end, Mr Ellis showed us his signals.

Ten minutes before the end, he was going to put one hand against his chin and the other over the edge of his high desk; and each minute he would close a finger or a thumb. That way, we'd know how long we'd got.

On the day, Dr Heywood came with a big silver watch. I was wearing a clean shirt, tie, jersey, knee socks and my best trousers, which were too small and hurt, and boy's knickers underneath made of yellow shiny string my mother had knitted specially, and a clean vest she'd sewn a silver thruppenny bit inside for luck; and she'd polished my clogs and combed my hair using water with sugar in to keep it flat.

Dr Heywood told us the rules and how long we had to answer the questions and asked us if we understood. Then he clicked his watch with his thumb, and we began.

The sums were hard, but the rest was easy and I finished and checked everything three times before

Mr Ellis started to bend his fingers until Dr Heywood clicked his watch again and said stop.

Then it was over, and we had the rest of the day off.

A few weeks later we got the results. Shirley, Angela, Roy, John and I had passed; but Sheila hadn't. Roger had. He was quite clever, but nobody had thought he would get through. Mr Ellis told the class the wrong one had won the place and it ought to have been Sheila.

Not much else happened.

There was Victory Sports Day on Norbury's Rec, which was a field where the village played football, and I won the Flat Boys Age 10 Running Race because I was used to it after being chased so much. I got half a crown for that.

Then there was a Fair. A tent had a sign outside it saying: HITLER'S SECRET WEAPON 1d. John and I paid the man at the entrance and went in.

People were standing around a box, and on top of it was a cage, and there was another sign saying the giant rat inside had been caught in the

Manchester Blitz, where it had been dropped by parachute with hundreds of others to eat babies and children.

It was brown and gnawing a turnip. It was about two feet long, with a tail as long again, and it had a white snout and huge bright orange teeth. But it wasn't a rat. It was a coypu. I told the man this, and he told me to shut my gob or else. But I told him coypus were from South America, not Germany, because I'd read about them; and they ate vegetables, not babies or children.

The man said he'd clip my ear hole, and John pulled me out of the tent and we ran. John called me daft. But I said it was a coypu. It really was.

And there was Empire Day. We had Prayers, then the whole school marched outside to the flagpole by the telephone exchange, and Canon Gravell came from the vicarage dressed in his white and black robes, and the Union Jack was hoisted up the flagpole and we saluted, the boys with their right hand and the girls with their left, and we sang 'God Save the King', 'Remember, Remember Empire Day, the

Twenty-fourth of May' and 'Onward, Christian Soldiers! Marching as to War'. I didn't know why we were singing it this year, now the war was over. Then Canon Gravell told us about Clive of India, and Gordon of Khartoum and other heroes, and he said prayers for them, and we said Amen and we went home.

Then it was the last day. John and I had planned what we were going to do.

It began with Twiggy leading Prayers. We knew we'd never have to hear him again. For him the summer holidays were five weeks, but we had seven before we started our new schools. It was the last dinnertime; the last playtime; the last whistle; the last bell.

Mr Ellis said goodbye and wished us luck.

We went out of the classroom for the last time; into the corridor for the last time. I looked up for the last time at the electric light bulb in the ceiling that was different from the others. It had a pointed tip, and Mr Noon said it was an original bulb, still working from the first day of the new extension my father had helped to build while he was in Pop Kennedy's class. And we went out of the door into the playground for the last time.

Between the school gateposts there was a strip of brass let into the ground; and this was our plan.

While we were on the playground side of the strip we were still at school. We would not have left until we had crossed it. We could cross; but Twiggy couldn't. He never could.

John and I held hands and ran. We ran from the playground, jumped over the brass, and were out; out under the sky and the white fluffy clouds with the gold and the glint of the weathercock burning to the wind.

DOWN MOSS
LANE

Bomb (1955)

Twelve years after finding the anti-personnel vitamin beverage bottle, with National Service in the
Royal Artillery behind me, I was conducting, illic-
itly, my first archaeological investigation on the
Edge. It was the Goldenstone.

The earliest surviving mention of the Goldenstone
is in a Perambulation, or record, of the boundary
and its marker points between the townships of
Over Alderley and Nether Alderley, made in 1598.
'... and so to the great stone called the golden stone
on the north side of the wain way ...'

I had been trying to find the wondrous-
sounding stone for a long time. Boundaries in
England are usually ancient and do not move. When

they were established they often incorporated features in the landscape as marker points because they were known and beyond dispute, and boundaries were the straight lines between. The Quest of the Goldenstone was important. It could be something very old.

When after many years I discovered the spot, a bank of earth had covered the stone, and I set about retrieving it with a pointing trowel and a soft brush, because that was what archaeologists did.

It soon became clear that the Goldenstone was old. It was a block of grey sandstone; not an outcrop, not golden, not even yellow, and dense with white

quartz pebbles. It had been brought from a distance, and showed no sign of metal tooling but had been shaped by battering with other stones. It turned out to be some twelve tons in weight. It would have needed time and effort to bring it here; which, along with the battering, suggested that it was perhaps prehistoric, possibly Bronze Age.

I worked slowly with trowel and brush. It took a fortnight.

In the second week I was trowelling down the western face of the stone, making a trench two feet wide to work in.

The tip of the trowel came up against something hard. I tapped. The sound was different. I abandoned the trowel and began to brush.

Aluminium and brass grew out of the sand. Engraved letters and numbers and a scaled band appeared … **208 MARK 6/2** … My guts cramped. I knew what it was, and what it meant.

I put the brush down gently, and rolled across the top of the Goldenstone to the other side and lay curled in a foetal position, eyes and mouth shut, my back to the stone, with my thumbs in my ears and my index fingers compressing my nostrils, as the army had taught.

Nothing happened. I snatched air. Nothing happened. I scurried in a crouch to the east of the Goldenstone and round in a wide arc to the trackway, straightened, and ran to Stormy Point and Saddlebole, down to Hough Lane and the police station.

I bashed opened the door. Sergeant Pessle looked up from his desk. I reverted to artillery jargon and shouted that I'd found Unexploded Ordnance, and told him to get the bomb squad immediately. Sergeant Pessle was not impressed.

I became more technical. I had unearthed a high-explosive three-seven Heavy Ack-Ack twenty-five-pounder shell with a mechanical two-zero-eight Mark six-two fuse; and it was armed. The timer had jammed. It was unstable and could explode at a touch.

Sergeant Pessle asked me where I had found it. I told him it was at the side of the track to Edge

House farm. He asked me how I had found it. I said I was digging. Digging what? The Goldenstone. A golden stone? he said. I repeated that it could explode at any time. The stone? he said. No; the shell. Sergeant Pessle supposed we had better go and have a look, then.

We went out and got into his black Morris Minor and drove up the hill. At The Wizard we turned off the road and bumped along the track for Edge House farm. At Seven Firs I told Sergeant Pessle to stop.

Sergeant Pessle asked what was wrong. I told him the Goldenstone was round the corner of the track ahead, on the left. He released the handbrake, but I said we had to stay there because the fragmentation shrapnel was lethal up to two hundred feet. He asked me what I expected him to do, and I told him again to get the bomb squad. He said there was no bomb squad, so I must show him.

I refused. He said I could suit myself, and got out of the car. I told him not to touch anything.

He set off along the track. I went and stood behind a tree. Sergeant Pessle reached the corner and stepped into my excavation. He held up the trowel and asked if this was all I'd got. He shook his head and knelt in the trench. I heard metal scrape on metal and shouted to him not to touch. He took no notice. He stood, dropped the trowel, bent down, wrenched and wrestled, and turned, holding the shell in his arms.

He laid the shell on the Goldenstone and came back to the car. I asked him what he was going to do. He said he was taking it to Wilmslow because there was a safe there.

He drove the car up to the Goldenstone, opened the boot, dumped the shell in, turned the car and came back. I ran to another tree. The shell was trundling around the floor of the boot and banging against the sides.

As he went past, Sergeant Pessle put his head out of the window. 'Eh. Alan,' he said. 'You do find 'em, don't you?'

St Mary's Vaccies (1974)

St Mary's Clyffe was turned into flats. Several years later it needed repairs, but it was found to be infected throughout with dry rot, and shortly afterwards the Gothic fantasy caught fire and blazed on its crag like the climax of a horror film. In its place was built something bland, not worthy of the setting; but I salvaged a spike of dragon tile.

Miss Turner wrote to me shortly before she retired. She was now the deputy head of a girls' school, and she wanted me to present the prizes at Speech Day. I had endured enough Speech Days to know that this was not something I could manage. But Miss Turner had asked. And Miss Turner was Miss Turner.

I arrived at the school. Miss Turner had aged, but not changed. I decided to do as she had done, so long ago. I would not be dull.

I presented the prizes; and then, a trick I'd learnt from seeing Danny Kaye at The London Palladium, I took a chair, turned it round, put it stage centre at the front, sat astride it, and told the story of the coal scuttle.

A few days later, a packet arrived by post. In it was a bar of Cadbury's Bournville Plain Chocolate, and a note in an unmistakeable hand, saying simply: 'Better now?'

I went to my workroom, shut the door, and ate the bar in one go.

The Nettling of Harold (2001)

I was by the Holy Well on the Edge, thinking, and did not want to be disturbed. The man's face was lined; the teeth were gappy, snaggled yellow. But I knew the grin; the eyes.

It was Harold.

My conveyor belt had taken me to Oxford. Harold's father was a general labourer, his brother Gordon a roofer. Harold's memory was of men coming home wet and exhausted, and he had been determined not to work outside. So he had become apprenticed to upholstery and undertaking. Now he was a psychiatric nurse caring for the criminally insane.

Harold told me what had happened more than half a century ago.

Our friendship had mattered to him. Although I was a sissy and a mardy-arse and one of 'Ellis's Pets' who got all the attention while the rest of the class were treated as rubbish, he and I had thought differently from the others. We talked differently and about different things; and I made him laugh. But the Belmont Gang played differently; and once I had gone he followed them.

He bunked off school with my cousin Geoffrey. They found it better to spend the day sitting in the dim of the school's disused air-raid shelters on cold benches, their feet on wet duckboards, learning to smoke the dib ends they picked up in the street, than to endure Twiggy's teaching.

Later, Harold's quality showed, and he was offered a place at Technical College. It was too late. 'When you've got five quid in your pocket on a Thursday,' he said, 'you want to be out with your mates at the weekend, not skint and stuck in the house with your nose in a book.'

But books drew him, and history was his need; history allied with travel. He was not a tourist. He went to see for himself what his reading had shown him. Scandinavian culture and archaeology were his special interests, along with the social history of his background and his innate knowledge of the Edge.

Harold

When Harold and I met at the Holy Well I was on the committee of The Alderley Edge Landscape Project, a ten-year multi-discipline investigation by The Manchester Museum and The National Trust of every aspect of the village, starting with the Early Triassic geology of two hundred and forty-five million years ago.

The committee consisted almost entirely of academics, who were strangers to the place. I was the only native; but I had been removed by education and life. My colleagues saw that the Project lacked an essential component: a member of the community capable of interpreting our work to the village; an advocate go-between.

Soon after the meeting at the Holy Well I knew that Harold was the one. He had spent his life within a quarter of a mile of where he was born; his connections with the culture of the adult Belmont Gang were unbroken; and he was articulate.

I reported back, and Harold was invited onto the committee.

The immediate reaction to his presence was alarm. Harold, through his time as a psychiatric nurse working with a team, knew how to function in committee. His ability was beyond doubt; but the form it took and the structure of its expression disturbed the academic mind. Where some followed the tradition of speaking with convoluted syntax through the Chair, Harold cut the flummery with wit. The committee learnt to beware of his flashing eye and grin. A few expressed unease in private that such a rough diamond had come among us and questioned the probity of his remarks. But Harold and his wisdom prevailed.

More, Harold was not prepared to accept the time limit of a decade on the Landscape Project. For him, Alderley and the Edge could not be opened and shut. He saw the continuity, and independently of the Museum he and his wife Margaret formed their own local history group, which flourished beyond the ten years of the Project and the further ten years of the preparation and publication of its Report.

On publication, the editor named Harold as a driving force of the Project. And at Harold's funeral, one of the academics thanked me for having urged his cause.

There is a dock for every nettle.